The Law of Capitalism and How to Transform It

New Legal Synthesis

Jedediah Britton-Purdy and David Grewal, editors

TITLES IN SERIES

The Law of Capitalism and How to Transform It
Katharina Pistor

The Law of Capitalism and How to Transform It

Katharina Pistor

Yale UNIVERSITY PRESS   New Haven and London

Published with assistance from the
Mary Cady Tew Memorial Fund.

Copyright © 2025 by Katharina Pistor.
All rights reserved.
This book may not be reproduced, in whole or in part, including illustrations, in any form (beyond that copying permitted by Sections 107 and 108 of the U.S. Copyright Law and except by reviewers for the public press), without written permission from the publishers.

Yale University Press books may be purchased in quantity for educational, business, or promotional use. For information, please e-mail sales.press@yale.edu (U.S. office) or sales@yaleup.co.uk (U.K. office).

Set in Caslon type by IDS Infotech, Ltd.
Printed in the United States of America.

Library of Congress Control Number: 2024952646
ISBN 978-0-300-28280-1 (hardcover)

A catalogue record for this book is
available from the British Library.

Authorized Representative in the EU: Easy Access System Europe, Mustamäe tee 50, 10621 Tallinn, Estonia, gpsr.requests@easproject.com

10 9 8 7 6 5 4 3 2 1

To my students

Contents

Preface / ix

CHAPTER 1
A Legal Regime / 1

CHAPTER 2
Theories of Capitalist Law / 21

CHAPTER 3
Legal Empowerment / 41

CHAPTER 4
Access to Legal Coercion / 66

CHAPTER 5
Legal Arbitrage / 83

CHAPTER 6
Rewiring the System / 102

CHAPTER 7
Beyond Capitalist Law / 117

Epilogue / 139

Notes / 145
Index / 187

Preface

This book emerged from a puzzle: Why is capitalism, a system that is coded in law, as I argued previously in *The Code of Capital*, so resistant to legal governance? Attempting to solve this puzzle required a deep dive into debates about law as a social system and into the specific characteristics of capitalist law and its normative underpinnings. This book describes my search for answers and the conclusions I have arrived at. Briefly summarized, capitalism's capacity to reconstitute itself in law, notwithstanding legal constraints that were put in place to contain it, follows largely from the duality of capitalist law: its separation into private and public law, each with different normative underpinnings and tools for realizing its goals. Private law is the main resource for coding capital and for constituting capitalism, and it benefits from the fact that, like public law, it too is law and is backed by the state's means of coercion. There is no such thing as ordering in private law that does not invoke at least the shadow of state power, even if we often pretend otherwise, and yet private law is firmly rooted in ideas of individual autonomy. Public law determines the scope of state power according to a set of normative principles set forth in a constitution, which may include individual rights but also commitments to collective self-governance as well as checks and balances on state power.

The reason that actors can employ private law to advance their interests even when doing so imposes costs on others or on society lies in three core characteristics of private law: (1) the legal empowerment of individual persons, both natural and legal; (2) their decentralized access to the consolidated means of coercion; and

(3) legal arbitrage, or the ability to repurpose the law for their own interests without losing its legal powers. These features share a common premise: the superiority of private ordering, idealized as self-ordering by free and autonomous individuals, to collective, or public, ordering, which is often demonized as top-down state intervention. And they operate to subordinate society to the market principle (as Karl Polanyi argued) or, perhaps more accurately, to private power wielders, who employ one part of the legal system, the private law, to undermine the reach and effectiveness of the other part, the public law.

This book strives to move beyond critique and to show that neither capitalism nor capitalist law are beyond reform. Elements for a genuine legal transformation can be found in existing law and practice and have the potential to bring about lasting change, provided that the law and legal practices are based on normative principles that respect others' quest for freedom. Because capitalism is ultimately a legal regime, law will be central in overcoming it, if only to create an economy that is stripped of the legal subsidies that the law has so readily afforded the holders of capital. An alternative strategy would be to break the legal system by revolutionary means and to impose a new regime in a top-down fashion. There are many reasons to shy away from such an approach, including the potential for violence that it would likely entail. Most importantly for the argument advanced here, it is simply not an option within a system that is derived from and evolves through law, because such a system will reconstitute itself even after a major shock, as it has done many times before. Seeking change through law does not make transformative change any easier, but arguably it makes it more likely—provided that there is a common understanding of the need for change and the importance of a coherent normative foundation that transcends the public-private divide. Ultimately, private law must be rooted in the same principles of social justice that animate democratic constitutionalism: most importantly, that power, no matter its origin (public or private), must be held to account and that its use must be limited to ensure that all have a fair chance to realize their life's goals alone or with others.

David Grewal was first in labeling capitalism a juridical regime. This idea has spread and has helped animate new lines of scholarship, including the "law and political economy" movement. I owe him and Jed Purdy, the two coeditors of this series, the inspiration for writing this book, and I am grateful to both for standing by from start to finish for conversations and critique. Many others, too many to be listed individually, helped along the way with questions, suggestions, comments, and critique in manuscript workshops, seminars, and faculty luncheons. I am deeply grateful for the time they put into reading earlier drafts, and I have tremendously benefited from my conversations with them. Of course, all the remaining errors and shortcomings are mine entirely.

Special thanks go to my research and faculty assistants who have worked long and hard to get this book to completion. Elise Zi Feng de Kleijn and Melanie Joy Mignucci helped identify case studies and select materials at different stages of this project, and Michael Paul McParlane copyedited every version of the manuscript with great care. Many thanks also to my editor, William Frucht, and the rest of the team at Yale University Press for bringing this book over the finish line. Thanks, too, to my copyeditor, Karen Schoen.

I am also grateful for the financial support from the Hewlett Foundation, which has allowed me to spend more time on this project than I otherwise could have, and to the Institute for Ideas and Imagination in Paris, which was an inspiring place to spend my sabbatical in 2022–23 and write parts of this book. The unsung hero of this book and so many other projects over the years is my husband, Carsten Bonnemann, whose love and support have always been unwavering even when my work imposed burdens on our time together.

I am dedicating this book to my students—past, present, and future—at Columbia Law School and elsewhere. Teaching is one of the most rewarding professions, especially when students are eager to learn but also critical about the materials presented to them. To me, teaching is all about learning from one another with respect and in the hope of achieving a better understanding of the world around us, a world that in many ways is shaped by law and by lawyers. I firmly believe that together we can forge a better law for a better world.

The Law of Capitalism and How to Transform It

I

A Legal Regime

Capitalism is a legal regime, not just an economic system as conventional wisdom has it.[1] Students of capitalism, from Karl Marx to Joseph Schumpeter and beyond, tend to associate capitalism with the trade of goods and services, labor relations, private ownership of the means of production, the business corporation, banking, and money—which are all regarded as economic phenomena.[2] In fact, these matters are legal to the core.[3] Trade and commerce rely on contract law, enterprises employ organizational law, ownership is determined by property law, and every "I owe you" worth its stated amount is an enforceable contract that may also enjoy the explicit or implicit backing of central banks, the issuers of the currency that serves as a unit of account, a means of exchange, and a store of value.[4]

In previous work, I have shown how capital is coded in law, or how specific legal modules—foremost among them property rights and collateral, contract, trust, corporate, and bankruptcy law—can be deployed to turn simple objects, claims, or ideas into capital.[5] Without legal coding, ordinary assets might still fulfill many purposes: land for grazing cattle or growing crops, or weaving machines for producing cloth, for example. But absent legal title, these objects may not be mortgaged or sold for profit and, as a result, will not produce wealth on the scale that legally coded capital assets can.

Explaining capital is one thing; understanding capitalism, a system, is another. It cannot be fully explained by the sum of all the legal modules that code capital. Instead, understanding capitalism requires lifting the gaze from the micro-institutional level where capital is coded to larger forces that are responsible for the interplay of law with politics and the economy, and to their normative underpinnings. Interestingly, the word *capitalism* has its own history quite distinct from "capital."[6] In the eighteenth century, the term was associated with state debt, which formed the core of the emergent capitalist regime.[7] People labeled *capitalists* were financiers who invested in the state debt that waxed and waned with the military adventures of the issuing sovereign. For the French political theorists who established the term *capitalism* in the vocabulary of political economy in the 1830s, capitalism stood for investing in state debt for private gain.[8] This captures the core logic of capitalism—the appropriation of social resources in pursuit of profits and wealth. After sovereign debt, the two major social resources that were appropriated were the legal and monetary systems.[9] They not only complement the natural resources that capitalism has claimed over the centuries—land, subsoil resources, animals, oceans, and the air we breathe—but also enable the appropriation of those resources. In short, I defined capitalism as a legal regime that enables the appropriation of collective resources, including the law itself, for private gain. Identifying law as both the resource and the means by which other resources are exploited is not tautological; it describes a regime that empowers (some) private actors to use private law to govern or even dominate others while also protecting these practices against state intervention with the help of public law.

Appropriation can take many different forms, brutal and subtle, direct and indirect. The former overlaps with what Marx called the "primitive" accumulation; the latter, with more sophisticated techniques that operate through legal means and are backed by state power. There is relatively little appropriation by physical force today. Instead, most takings by private actors are cloaked in law—in rights and claims that are based in property rights or contracts and are enforceable in a court of law. This is possible because capitalist law prioritizes private over public ordering and largely exempts private parties from respecting others' individual rights enshrined in constitutional law.[10] And critically, the law has institutionalized these priorities by empowering private actors to take the law into their own hands; by ensuring that they have access to the centralized means of coercion to enforce their rights; and by tolerating legal arbitrage as an expression of individual autonomy even when this comes at the expense of the rights of others. Each of these three features is capable of biasing the legal system in favor of capitalism; in combination, they have deeply entrenched the interests of the wielders of private power and subordinated much of the law to their interests.

The aim of this book is not primarily to offer yet another critical analysis of capitalism or capitalist law. The parts that provide the diagnosis are meant to offer insights into capitalism's inner workings and to develop a strategy to move beyond this regime. Capitalism is often defended as a system that has elevated people out of poverty like no other.[11] It may have flaws, but they should and could be fixed because there is ultimately no real alternative.[12] Moreover, in light of its accomplishments, many often assume that capitalism offers solutions for the biggest challenges we face today: the threats that emanate from climate change and the erosion of democratic self-governance. More capital and more growth are the standard answers offered.[13] Yet these (existential) problems are products of capitalism, a regime that has provided incentives for individual autonomy and entrepreneurship as harbingers of growth but that has also treated nature, people, and social resources as inputs for a profit machine that knows no limits, not even in the face of ecocide, the extinction of entire species and ecological systems. It is hard to believe that the same system that is responsible for these problems can also solve them.

Understanding capitalism as a legal regime might suggest that leaving it behind is next to impossible because at every step along the way legally protected interests will block change. However, it also points to the possible levers and directions of change. A legal regime is a matter of human choice, though not of grand design; it is the product of the many choices that people make as individuals and as members of families, communities, and the polity they are a part of. If that is so, different choices are at least imaginable as individuals and collectives weigh in on the use and interpretation of existing law, imagine different uses, and even mobilize for formal legal change. It also follows from the premise that capitalism is a legal regime that a transformative change is possible only through law. For transformative change, isolated alterations to existing laws or institutions will not be enough. Instead, it requires putting private law on normative foundations that are compatible with and supportive of the norms that animate constitutional democracy, including respect for human dignity, accountability, and collective self-governance.

For advocates of capitalism, this system stands for individual initiative and financial rewards for taking risks when making bets on an unknown future.[14] Too little attention is given in this account to how systematically prioritizing individual autonomy and private over collective ordering might be incompatible with freedom and justice for all. Because the individual is the most vulnerable unit in society, it makes sense to start with the individual in any theory of social justice. But it can hardly serve as justification for legally empowering some to impose their will on others without appropriate checks and balances. People can make promises to each other and exchange goods and services, but which of these promises enjoy the authority of the law is a matter of social, not private, choice. Yet in capitalist regimes private actors play an outsize role in making this choice, and most seek to advance their own interests with little regard for social justice.

To be effective, a legal order must enjoy sufficient authority so that most people will respect the outcome it produces, even if they lose. A law that empowers without accountability, that creates rights without obligations and enriches without levying liabilities, is in danger of losing its legitimacy and can hardly be defended as just. It may be kept in place by a mix of ideology and coercion, but it loses its greatest asset, legitimacy, and, as a result, voluntary compliance. The recent rise of populism in many capitalist countries poses a threat to democracy, but the tolerance for lawlessness that some leaders of these movements display is also a threat to the very legal order that enables capitalism.[15] Capitalism has always been characterized by deep contradictions, as Marx and Friedrich Engels noted. The reason that it has not yet succumbed to those contradictions lies in the willingness of societies to mobilize social resources whenever a crisis threatens capitalism's future.[16] The key resources employed, law and money, may appear to be infinite, but they are not.[17] Their availability and impact depend on the continued political support for the authority of the law and the institutions of the state that uphold it.

The future of capitalism is not just a matter of political or economic battles; it has become a battle with nature itself. For a system that is based on relentless expansion, the confrontation with a bounded natural system poses an existential threat for both. Capitalism has survived on the illusion that there would always be sufficient social resources and political goodwill to ensure its survival. Nature will be less forgiving. Humans have altered nature to a point that justifies the label "the Anthropocene" for our age, but this does not mean that humans are able to escape nature's wrath, as demonstrated by the increase in the destructive forces of wildfires, droughts, and floods related to climate change.[18]

It is not an accident that capitalism co-evolved with the rise of the modern state. As states solidified, local markets were integrated into national economies, not simply by natural evolution but by mobilizing public power to actively break down legal barriers to trade and commerce and by constructing legal systems at the local, national, and international levels. The great social transformation that paved the way to modernity began, in Polanyi's account, with the elimination of Elizabethan poverty laws and the busting of guilds. It set the stage for the subordination of society to the market principle against which societies rebelled in the early decades of the twentieth century only to be subordinated once again in the later ones.[19]

Just as markets were pried open for capitalist endeavors at home, European powers burst open foreign markets with military force in the name of development and destroyed ancient civilizations that stood in the way of colonization.[20] They chartered trading companies that were run by private actors for profit and armed them with guns and the legal authority to govern the people conquered by the colonizing powers.[21] These companies brought with them the law of the states that chartered them, which they used to assert private property rights, to enter into deals with locals, and, using the newly established courts, to enforce their claims against those locals.[22]

Colonialism was not lawless but it did display law's power over entire peoples whose own systems of social ordering were derided as uncivilized.[23] Neither was colonial law only or even primarily about administrative or public law by a foreign state. Private law played a critical role, and not only in settlers' colonies or to their benefit.[24] Property rights vested the colonizers with control rights over resources, and debt contracts ensured that even rich locals became increasingly dependent on foreign creditors. Only the latter had access to the high-powered money of their own sovereign back in London or Paris, which enabled them to weather financial crises that arose, while locals often succumbed to those crises.[25]

The end of colonialism also did not mark the end of the imposed law. Most former colonies kept the private law of their former colonial masters, even if they wrote new constitutions and abolished administrative laws and regulations that were used to suppress locals.[26] And as foreign trade and investment became global, the laws of the leading capitalist economies, the United Kingdom and the United States, came to dominate international trade, investment, and the global financial system.[27] In the postcolonial setting, conquest and the imposition of foreign law by force was no longer an option, but this did not stop the transplantation of law from the core to the periphery of the increasingly global capitalist system. It was not the logic of the regime but the means that changed for imposing foreign law when financial support for less developed countries was conditioned on the adoption of the "best practice" rules of "advanced" economies.[28] In short, capitalism owes its global expansion not to an open and fair competition of alternative systems; it has been coded in law with both pressure and massive financial support from multilateral institutions and capitalist countries.

Given the centrality of law to the capitalist project, it is critical to understand its peculiar capitalist qualities. Would any law be amenable to capitalism, or are there specific features that make it so? These questions are rarely asked by lawyers. In capitalist economies, law tends to be treated as neutral, as an impartial system, the primary function of which is to maintain social order and protect private property and the sanctity of contracts.[29] By contrast, socialist legal theorists, from Marx to Evgeny Pashukanis, have argued that law reflects the socioeconomic conditions—in particular, capital's control over the means of production—and therefore that in communism, the state and its law would wither away to give rise to a system that was no longer dependent on either.[30] Economists have also been less shy than lawyers about identifying features of legal systems that can be described as distinctively capitalist. They have taken John Maynard Keynes's insight that capitalism is essentially about investment and extended it to include the need to legally protect investor rights, but little else.[31]

In fact, law does not only protect but also empowers and provides the tools with which new capital assets can be coded. Nowhere is this more apparent than in the case of financial assets, which are creatures of contracts, property rights, and collateral law and are issued and traded by legal entities and backstopped by state-issued money. These legal devices fuel capital and create private wealth, but they come at a cost: They deepen inequality and add to the precarity of life for people who rarely benefit from the inflation of financial asset prices but often bear the brunt of subsequent downturns.[32] The rise of the regulatory state can be explained as an attempt to mitigate the externalities that capitalism creates in what has aptly been called a "risk society."[33] Banks and securities markets were among the first targets of state regulation.[34] These attempts to tame capitalism did not prevent the economic crises of the late 1920s and 1930s, but did strengthen the case for more regulation after these crises had subsided.[35] The United States enacted the New Deal, a comprehensive package of reforms that was geared primarily toward banking and securities markets but that also included financial support for homeowners and small businesses. These measures put the capitalist system on a more stable and more equitable path. After World War II, the financial system was also placed on more stable footing: Coordination, not competition, became the new paradigm for governing foreign-exchange relations under the leadership of the newly established International Monetary Fund (IMF) in the Bretton Woods system.[36] With the dollar pegged to gold, all other major currencies pegged to the dollar, and capital controls firmly in place, financial stability was all but ensured. The fact that this curtailed financial activity was deemed a price worth paying at the time.

However, within a few decades the same regulatory means were deemed repressive.[37] Even before regulatory restrictions were relaxed, many safeguards that had been put in place to contain financial capital were eroded.[38] Legal engineering weakened capital controls long before the gold standard was abandoned by the United States in 1971, paving the way for the free movement of capital and a much looser regulatory regime.[39] Private actors in pursuit of profit opportunities devised swaps to exploit loopholes in the legal scaffolding that was established to maintain the system of capital controls and benefited from regulatory forbearance when offering dollar-denominated bank accounts in offshore jurisdictions.[40] In effect, the coordination of global capital flows was taken out of the hands of the IMF and handed over to markets as regulators in the United States and the United Kingdom, the heartlands of global finance, looked the other way.

The ways in which finance escaped regulatory controls within decades after they had been put in place illustrate the interplay of the two bodies of capitalist law: public and private. Simply put, public law is the law that governs state actions, or the vertical relation between the state and its citizens; by contrast, private law governs the horizontal relation between free and autonomous individuals. The ideas about private law's freedom-enhancing powers were forged in the nineteenth century as an antidote to the state's greater involvement in social and economic affairs.[41] In the 1920s and 1930s, however, legal scholars questioned the public-private divide more fundamentally, noting that in the end, all law requires state backing, and challenged spheres of autonomy under private law that could be freely exploited by powerful private actors.[42] Viewed in this light, all law is public.[43]

This conclusion, however, overlooks the fact that the reach of public law into spheres of private law is deeply contested. Although there is always a possibility that the state will legislate or regulate to restrict private actions, such restrictions can be and often are legally challenged by private actors. Even more importantly, this conclusion ignores the perspective of those who are being governed by private actors through law. As Elizabeth Anderson has explained, "[T]he privacy of a government is defined relative *to the governed*, not relative to the state."[44] To the governed, private government distinguishes itself by keeping them out of decision-making. It is the kind of government that existed in pre-republican times, when authority could not be questioned without fear of repercussions and participation in government was reserved for a few loyalists or subjects who were too powerful to ignore.[45] Importantly, private government is also made in law. The state sanctions corporations that assert control over labor and has on occasion allowed the invocation of antitrust or property law against labor unions. For the governed, whether they are subject to private or public governance is less important than the immediate reality they face: being dominated by wielders of power (individuals, but more frequently corporations) who are not answerable to them.

Private-law theorists offer a radically different account of private law. They emphasize freedom over state tutelage and individual autonomy over collective needs. Hanoch Dagan and Avihay Dorfman, who are in the progressive wing of legal liberalists, define *private law* as "the law that governs our horizontal interactions in a variety of settings where we encounter other persons in our capacity as persons rather than as citizens or, more generally, as members of a political community."[46] Like Anderson, Dagan and Dorfman reject the conventional distinction between private and public law that focuses primarily on the role of the state. Whereas for Anderson the perspective of the governed takes center stage, for Dagan and Dorfman it is the relation of free individuals, each in pursuit of their legitimate goals but bound to one another by mutual respect.

The critical question is which of these accounts more accurately reflects relations among nominally private parties—that is, individuals or entities that do not occupy state offices—under capitalism. In my assessment, the notion of private government is closer to empirical reality than the idea of persons meeting each other as autonomous beings in a space outside polities and communities. It may be true that some legal institutions in existing law reflect the normative ideals that Dagan and Dorfman amplify in their interpretative theory of private law. However, most transactions that most people face on a daily basis are not person-to-person. They are between natural persons and legal persons and are governed by contracts that are not the product of equal and fair bargaining between the two parties to it but are standard contracts that the stronger party imposes on the weaker. The same holds for the global sphere, where multinational corporations, not individual entrepreneurs, set the terms for global supply chains and even for the governments of countries where they operate as foreign investors.

In fact, with the help of the three characteristics of capitalist law that I identified earlier—private legal empowerment, decentralized access to the centralized means of coercion, and legal arbitrage—private law served as a weapon in dismantling the safeguards against capitalism that had been put in place after World War II. The first, legal empowerment, recognizes the fact that the law endows private actors with the power to use it to advance their own interests, even at the expense of others. The law establishes minimum conditions for making a contract or a property right enforceable but leaves the rest to private parties, who are "free" to use the law in ways that maximize their interests.

The hallmark of modern statehood is that it has centralized the means of physical coercion, but this does not mean that only state actors have access to these means. The success of legal adventures, and the expansion of markets they beget, hinges on the commitments that private actors make to one another being binding, or enforceable, in a court of law. The second feature of capitalist law, litigation, is the means by which parties can access the centralized means of coercion, and that allows parties with the right resources to engage in practices that in their most extreme form at times amount to lawfare:[47] They sue others defensively, push the limits of the law in the hope that challengers will not bother to sue them, or use their bargaining power to reduce the risk of being sued by others by including waivers or mandatory arbitration clauses.

Legal arbitrage, the third feature, shows how actors with greater resources can engineer end runs around the law. Law is inevitably incomplete and therefore leaves ample room for interpretation, for exploiting gaps, and for drawing analogies, even when this pulls the law away from its original purpose.[48] Legal-arbitrage opportunities are particularly rampant when different legal or regulatory regimes overlap, as they necessarily do in federalist systems—for example, at the intersection of private and public law, as well as in transnational transactions, which tend to involve more than one jurisdiction. When legal systems give private actors the power to choose the legal regime to be applied to their private transactions, legal arbitrage can be taken to another level altogether. As more and more countries expanded the choice set for private actors, these actors took advantage of the possibility to pick and choose among different legal systems and apply the one that best fit their needs to their contracts, business organizations, and tax or regulatory regime. In theory, anybody can take advantage of legal arbitrage, but in practice, it benefits actors with sufficient resources to hire attorneys to help them navigate a maze of domestic and international laws in order to configure a world of law that works best for them.

Jointly, these three features of capitalist law help capitalism circumvent the legal constraints that were established to guard against its excesses or protect aspects of social life from being subordinated to its logic: the primacy of profit maximization over all other values. Attempts to regulate capitalism through legislative intervention—for example, by empowering labor or by using the tax system to redistribute some of its gains—have not been without success. But they have not stemmed the tide of capitalist expansion and subordination, because their effects have often been muted by legal counterstrategies. Once a matter that has been regulated fades from public attention or a crisis subsides, attorneys develop new strategies for their clients in private law that help avoid the reach of public law and regulation. As more actors join the trend, it is only a matter of time before capitalism ramps up again. The forces at work are always the same: individual empowerment against collective decision-making, combined with decentralized access to coercion and rampant legal arbitrage justified by ideas of the primacy of private over public governance. And these forces have allowed capitalism to free itself from legal constraints time and again.

The relation between (formal) law and (informal) norms has always been an uneasy one. Critics of the state accuse it of arbitrary rulemaking that conflicts with the norms societies are quite capable of developing on their own. In the words of Friedrich Hayek, "[l]aw is older than the state," which is to say that law does not need a state and is ultimately better fashioned from below.[49] Not all bottom-up lawmaking is normatively appealing, however. Social norms and conventions often entrench relations of power that the weaker members of society may find difficult to escape, leaving them bereft of means to challenge the established order. The ability of women to control their bodies, to name just one example, remains precarious in most societies around the globe because the law is made or interpreted to (re-)align with patriarchal norms.[50]

In formal legal systems, deliberate lawmaking has been separated from social norms, and this has made it possible to some degree to create alternatives to, complement, or override custom.[51] Modern states became legal modernizers in more than one way. They endorsed the idea of individual rights that were untethered from social status. Private law, which preceded the modern nation-states and democratic constitutionalism, was incorporated into the constitutional orders that emerged from the struggles with absolutist rulers, oftentimes sight unseen. In this way, legal claims that existed in private law were endorsed as constitutional rights that could be enforced not only against other private parties but also against the state. Individual empowerment through constitutional law may have been intended as a check on state power and the danger of its abuse. But these legal empowerments also sowed the seeds for the rise of private power in the hands of those who knew how and had the resources to use these legal empowerments to expand their control over others. Lacking are checks on wielders of private power similar to those that are used to hold state power at bay. In the United States, in particular, constitutional norms have been repurposed to empower corporations to claim as legal *persons* rights that were created for humans and, more specifically, for freed slaves; corporations asserted and were granted a right to property as a shield against regulation and a right to free speech to finance election campaigns, and convinced courts to rule that legislation that gave labor unions access to employers' premises must be struck down as an expropriation without compensation.[52]

The failure of rights-based legal systems to create just law has been widely noted in the literature.[53] Rights "went wrong," as my colleague Jamal Greene has argued in the American context.[54] He blames an overly formalistic approach to the conception of rights by the U.S. Supreme Court that privileges some "fundamental" rights over others without recognizing the need to balance all rights. One may take this critique even a step further. The insistence on private rights without effective checks and balances has enabled the rise of private power without effective legal constraints. A mere fig leaf of consent, granted hastily by clicking "agree" on a website, or by signing where stickers were already inserted in documents that are too long to read and too complicated to understand, is the mechanism by which millions endorse private government.

State power has been subject to many more constraints, at least in constitutional democracies. Elections should not be mistaken for democracy, but they are one of many mechanisms to hold officeholders to account. Others include the division of power into three separate branches—the executive, the legislature, and the judiciary—and the protection of individual rights that can be mobilized against the state, to name just the most common. By comparison, there are far fewer options to contain private power. Litigation is an option, but its costs often operate as a deterrent, standing rules limit access to the courts, and mandatory arbitration clauses can deny access altogether.[55] Private actors are not alone in the fight against private power; states can be mobilized against it too. The most powerful weapons that states have devised to directly control private power are taxation and antitrust law, fines, and criminal sanctions, but they are limited in scope and effectiveness, and states often lack the resources to effectuate them or fear a backlash from capital that might move to more accommodating jurisdictions. Moreover, they do not address the root causes of the power balance but merely seek to constrain it ex post, which is often too late.

Power and the possible abuse of power have been the primary concerns of political theorists since the Enlightenment. Private agents may not command the means of physical coercion that states do, but "private government" is often experienced as just as oppressive as state government by those who are subjected to it.[56] A just law would instead require accountability of all power wielders. This, I shall argue, requires a different normative foundation for private law and complementary institutions to guard it. The powers of private actors must be limited by the rights of others, and rights must be paired with the reciprocal obligation to ensure that others have similar options to advance their interests and do not have to live by the dictates of the more powerful. This idea is reflected in the "human capabilities" approach that Amartya Sen and Martha Nussbaum developed, which I build on in the last chapter of the book to chart a path beyond capitalist law.[57]

Human capabilities are appeals not just to a state or single society to provide the conditions that enable others to live lives they have reason to value. Under capitalist law, private actors escape obligations they owe others and society at large because they combine their economic prowess with legal empowerment, access to the means of coercion, and legal arbitrage to legitimize and entrench their might. The flip side of this is that others—in fact, the majority of people—are denied similar opportunities. They are often subjected to the rule of others without being able to hold them to account.[58]

This book builds on a long history of critiques of capitalism. The literature can be roughly divided into three main camps: Marxism, Keynesianism, and institutionalism, each of which has many subgroups within it. Scholars committed to one school of thought often embrace some arguments that are central to another. This makes classification difficult and easy to challenge. Nonetheless, it might be helpful to state what I take to be the core contributions of each camp and how my own approach relates to them.

Marxism remains the dominant vantage point for critiques of capitalism. Marx and Engels never developed a full theory of the state and the law, but their ideas about the state and the law can be distilled from their writings.[59] Class struggle, particularly the antagonism between labor and capital, is central. Power relations and attention to the material conditions they reflect are the lasting and arguably most important contribution of Marxist scholarship. Only by overcoming the material conditions that enable capitalism can these power struggles be overcome. In recent decades, scholars in the Marxist tradition have begun to question the relative importance of labor in late capitalist societies, pointing to technological change that eliminates many jobs and demands new explanations other than the exploitation of labor as the source of surplus that capital extracts.[60] Marxist scholars have also revived the debate about the relation between politics and the economy and have moved decisively beyond the crude idea of the state and its laws as merely instruments of power in the hands of the ruling class. Instead, researchers have attempted to explain the *relative* autonomy of the law and the state in existing capitalist regimes.

For Keynesians, the economy, its productivity, and the role of money and finance in investment take center stage.[61] Power relations recede into the background, and the state and its laws are implied but not central for the analysis of the driving forces of capitalism. A partial exception is Hyman Minsky, who was keenly aware of the importance of law for structuring a financial system that he described as inherent to capitalism but also inherently unstable.[62] He even developed a legal-reform agenda that targeted the financial system as well as the corporate sector and competition law in his attempt to develop a more stable economy.[63] Centering the analysis of capitalism on money and finance remains the major contribution of Keynesianism and led to Minsky's insight that capitalism is essentially a financial system, albeit a different one from the ideals of modern finance.[64] It shifted the focus of economic analysis from production to investment, and from the antagonism between capital and labor to a more complex understanding of the relation between what Marx called "circular" capital, on one hand, and society at large, on the other.[65]

The third camp, institutionalism, encompasses a range of approaches that derive their understanding of capitalism from the analysis of its most prevalent institutions, including property rights, the corporation, money, and credit. Leading contributions include Max Weber's sociology of law, as well as the "old" institutionalists like John Commons and Thorstein Veblen and legal realists such as Robert Hale.[66] In their view, law, which Veblen called the "working rules of society," was critical for understanding the logic of socioeconomic systems. Theirs was an inductive approach that was aimed at unearthing the operation of law in society and that also shed a critical light on how some institutions undermined the prospects of freedom and equality, themes that would be picked up again in the critical legal studies movement of the 1970s.[67] By contrast, the new institutional economics, associated with economists like Douglass North and Oliver Williamson, has idealized private property rights and contracts in particular as harbingers of economic efficiency, the gold standard for assessing institutions, especially in the neoliberal era.[68] Other institutionalists, including Geoffrey Hodgson, have returned to an evolutionary or, like Wolfgang Streeck, a Marxist tradition that depicts institutions as reflecting underlying social dynamics, including class struggles.[69] These different schools of thought are united in their interest in institutions as elements of social orders—their origin, their evolution, and how they shape expectations, behavior, and outcomes. These different branches of institutionalist analysis agree that institutions pervade all aspects of society and the economy, as well as the political system, but they have different views on the genesis of institutions (emergence vs. design), their propensity to change over time (path dependence vs. continuous change), and their role in shaping versus merely reflecting relations of power and dependency.

Institutionalism is therefore better described as an approach for understanding complex social systems rather than a full-blown social theory.[70] Depending on the questions posed and the theoretical leaning of the researcher, the outward extension from institutions to the broader social system they constitute and within which they operate might focus on markets, firms, or political entities, or might emphasize rationality, efficiency, or power relations. In short, using institutions as the starting point of one's analysis does not determine any of these choices or replace debates over social norms and social goals.

My own approach takes a variant of institutionalism—namely, "legal institutionalism"—as a starting point, but imbued with a strong dose of political economy.[71] Institutions are not neutral, but reflect and are arguably even constitutive of power relations. I believe that there is value in examining social systems from a legal vantage point—not because all social life is determined by law, nor because law is a superior form for organizing societies as compared with informal rules.[72] Rather, I am convinced that social systems that employ law are different from social systems that prioritize informal social norms over formal law, and thus warrant special attention. Formal legal systems employ an entire apparatus of lawmakers, law interpreters, and law enforcers who use law to shape social relations, not directly through, but in the shadow of, the coercive powers of the state. The legal system institutionalizes these powers and determines who can mobilize them and to what ends. It constitutes both public and private power and constrains the former in particular. How it does this, who determines the content and meaning of legal rules, and who benefits and loses as a result are the questions that a political economy of law can help answer.

With this book I hope not only to offer a deeper understanding of capitalist law, which has been foundational to capitalism and has secured its dominance for centuries, but also to chart pathways beyond this system. The analysis therefore combines diagnostics with normative goals, as well as directions for normative and institutional change. At the same time, it eschews the temptation of developing a utopia for life after capitalism. Utopias have not fared well as predictors of actual future change, and not only has the major anti-capitalist utopia—namely, communism—failed, but its interim state, Soviet-style socialism, has been deeply disappointing. Real existing capitalism or socialism, however, are not the only possible ways for organizing socioeconomic systems. Liberating us from this binary choice is the first step for considering alternatives to either system and charting a path for social justice through law.[73]

The road map for the book is as follows. Chapters 2 through 5 offer a diagnosis of capitalist law, including legal theories (chapter 2), and a critical analysis of the core features of capitalist law—namely, private legal empowerment (chapter 3), decentralized access to the state's coercive powers (chapter 4), and legal arbitrage (chapter 5). That is followed by a discussion of the kind of transformative change that is needed, which, as I will argue, must center on the law (chapter 6). The last chapter (chapter 7) seeks to chart a path beyond capitalism by showing how a shift in its normative foundations might help trigger a deep transformation from within.

2

Theories of Capitalist Law

Is there such a thing as a capitalist law? This question is rarely asked today. Legal and political theorists are more interested in developing general theories of law, the state, or the market, and they are prone to adding qualifiers to these theories to account for variations on the theme—for example, the "neoliberal" state or the "social welfare" state. Similarly, economists tend to equate capitalism with a market economy without considering that a free-market exchange of goods and services does not have to entail privileging capital over other interests as a matter of law. Indeed, a genuine market economy would require a level playing field that denied capital the legal privileges it has come to take for granted. By contrast, legal theorists in the Marxist tradition have long argued that there cannot be a general theory of the state, law, or the economy, because these systems are invariably shaped by power relations, economic conditions, and ideologies that make them distinctive—in this case, distinctively capitalist.[1]

Classical and neoclassical economic theories have little toleration for how the law constitutes economic relations and instead treat it as external to the market economy. This became painfully obvious when economists turned from theory to policy and advised the former socialist countries on their "transition" to a market economy. They assumed that there was a relatively straight path from socialism to capitalism and that this path involved little more than getting the state out of the economy and allowing market forces to take over.[2] Yet, over three decades after the demise of Soviet-style socialism, most countries in the region still struggle with developing legal orders that reflect the normative aspirations and preferences of their citizens. The idea that markets and democracy belonged together was a credo of the 1990s, which helped justify radical economic reforms even as societies struggled to ensure that they would finally have a say in their future. This is perhaps best exemplified by Hungary and Poland, the two countries that were widely perceived to be the success stories of the former socialist world's embrace of capitalism and democracy.[3] Yet these two countries have been engulfed by authoritarian populism that produced hostility toward the rule of law and the broader economic order of the European Union, the very institutions they eagerly embraced when the old socialist regime crumbled.[4]

Karl Polanyi would not have been surprised. He identified the subordination of society to the market principle as one of the root causes for the backlash against democratic constitutionalism and the rise of communism and fascism in the first part of the twentieth century.[5] However, his hope that the end of World War II would bring about another "great transformation" that would more firmly embed the market and its institutions in society has not been realized.[6] Instead, capitalism successfully unleashed itself from restrictions that were established after World War II, including capital controls and a greater assertion of public over private law domestically and internationally. And once unleashed in the core capitalist regimes—the United States and the United Kingdom—it expanded to other parts of the globe, leaving hardly a country untouched.

The idea that capitalist forces could be contained by public law assumes a high degree of autonomy of the state from private power and, in the international realm, the capacity of a plurality of states to coordinate their actions to overcome the limitations of their own territorially bounded power. More than this, it assumes that public law has priority over private law, when in fact private law is the source code for capital and capital has access to the state's enforcement powers to impose its will on others.

Private law predates the modern state. More than this, constitutional democracies embraced the private legal order they inherited and granted constitutional protection to private property without defining its content and scope along with other civil and political rights. This shielded private actors from overt threats by the state to the riches they amassed with the help of the state's law and enforcement apparatus. Over time, these shields have also been used to push back against attempts by the state to protect society from private power, from being subordinated once more to the market. Further, the interpretation of individual rights as natural rights has fostered the idea that property rights are "natural," in contrast to the rules and regulations that the state, an artificial construct, imposes on society.

In fact, capitalism is itself a product of law. Armed with the tools of private law, well-positioned and well-resourced actors have been able to code new assets as capital and push the frontiers of rights while pushing back against obligations and avoiding liability for harm they inflict on others. The system is perpetually in search of new resources that can be coded as capital, and its expansive logic and reliance on credit to leverage investments into an unknown future implies that capitalism is inherently fragile. Capitalism frequently does find itself on the brink of collapse from which it can be rescued only by mobilizing social resources—in particular, state-issued money. This has major ramifications not just for the constitution of markets but also for the shape of politics and society. Law is both the cloth from which capital is cut and the means by which democracies govern themselves, institutionalize power, and legitimize the use of coercion.[7] It follows that capitalism is not simply an economic system that fuels investment, as Keynesians suggest, or an assemblage of institutions that shape the economy, as new institutional economists argue, but a social system that is imbued with power, which has been institutionalized as law. It is therefore critical to obtain a better understanding of the interrelation of the state, the law, and the economy in capitalist regimes.

Legal scholars from within the capitalist system have only rarely analyzed their law as capitalist or highlighted the legal system's distinct capitalist features, notwithstanding the fact that some legal codes are explicitly labeled "bourgeois"—like the German *Bürgerliche Gesetzbuch*. The assumption that law is neutral stands in the way of such a recognition. Even the field of comparative law, which is more attuned to differences between legal cultures, has largely avoided the label *capitalist law* and has stuck to the term *private law*. It has divided the world into different legal systems—the civil-law and the common-law families—but without drawing a clear connection between the legal family and the capitalist system it organizes.[8] Socialist law was added to the genealogy of legal families only belatedly and without an attempt to overhaul the existing classification by legal origin along political-economic lines, and the socialist legal family was scrapped soon after the demise of Soviet-style socialism.[9]

By contrast, the early twentieth century witnessed a vigorous debate about the nature of capitalist law even in the West, but more so in post-revolutionary Russia.[10] Two leading socialist theorists offered disputed alternative perspectives on capitalist law: Karl Renner, an Austrian legal theorist and politician, and Evgeny Pashukanis, a Russian theorist of socialist law. Both were deeply influenced by historical materialism but drew different conclusions from it.

Renner argued that the state emerges from society and, in the case of capitalism, from hierarchically structured social relations.[11] He agreed with Marx that the law of property reflects, but does not cause, social relations of power. In the ideal state of the world, which Renner (like Engels before him) associated with the period of simple commodity production, the law and the underlying socioeconomic conditions would be fully aligned.[12] Under capitalism, by contrast, they diverge and produce two distinct types of property, one legal and the other economic.[13] "Economic property," Renner wrote, "the essence of which is the capital function, need not necessarily coincide with the legal property."[14] Economic property often moves beyond legal property and transforms a simple right to a thing (a right *in rem*) into a complex set of social relations.[15] Importantly, this transformation occurs largely without explicit legislative change, but instead by the reinterpretation and repurposing of existing law.

Renner therefore likened law to an empty vessel that can be filled with different content in accordance with underlying economic conditions. Property rights are not always the same; their content varies by economic regime. It is not the law as such that causes a particular allocation of economic power, but economic power relations that give a particular content to the law. Judges often play a critical role in sanctioning the economic transformation of property rights as legal: "Even the law treats the capital function as a special quality of the object," Renner wrote.[16]

Responding to Renner's theory of private law, Pashukanis dismissed this analysis because of Renner's openness of law to different contents as his positivist inclinations.[17] By contrast, for Pashukanis it was not the substance but the *form* of law that rendered all law inherently capitalist and, as such, incapable of being filled with new substance.[18] The notion of *legal* rights and *legal* subjectivity, together with the fetishization of formal *legal* equality, were the source of hierarchy and material inequality in capitalism. For Pashukanis, hierarchy does not create law but instead is a product of a particular form of law—namely, the commodity form.[19] This form finds its origin in the commodity exchange combined with the idea that humans are themselves defined as legal persons and that their relations to others, to objects, and to nature are all determined by a legal system that reduces them to commodities.[20]

An essential feature of capitalist law, according to Pashukanis, is the separation of law into private and public law. "Subjective law is the primary law, for it is based, after all, on material interest, which exists independently of the external, or conscious, regulation of social life," he wrote.[21] The idea of legally protected individual interests (or subjective rights) can be traced all the way back to Roman times. When translated into constitutional law, individual rights enter the realm of the political, where they are hailed as freedom-enhancing. Yet, according to Pashukanis, constitutions are only "a reflection of the private-law form in the sphere of political organization."[22] They pit material individual interests against collective interests and subordinate the latter to the former. In short, constitutionalism and rule-of-law talk merely disguise the fact that "[t]he power of one person over another is brought to bear in reality as the force of law, that is to say as the force of an objective, impartial norm."[23]

By contrast, contemporary legal realists argued that all law is essentially public because even private law is ultimately backed by state power.[24] Pashukanis retorted that one might just as well say that "all state law was once private law."[25] The critical point is that law was once unified whereas modern law is characterized by the duality of private and public law, which first emerged in the cities of the Middle Ages. "It is there that the material and personal obligations pertaining to land disintegrate . . . into taxes and obligations in favor of the municipality on the one hand, and into rent used on private property on the other," Pashukanis stated.[26] The separation of rights from substance and the elevation of individual rights over collective interests engendered capitalist law. Pashukanis's commodity-form theory of law helps explain how material conditions shape law, but also how law reframes social relations as legal relations of formally equal legal subjects. In his work, he stressed historical materialism as the foundation of his analysis, but this did not prevent him from veering into institutionalist territory by recognizing the framing power of law.

Theorizing about capitalist law did not end with the works of Renner and Pashukanis, but for decades it occupied only a niche space in legal scholarship and thought.²⁷ In the Soviet Union, Stalinism put an end to the lively debate about the nature of law in the 1920s; many of its leading participants, among them Pashukanis, were executed. Within capitalism, voices that viewed law as foundational to capitalism, such as the institutionalist John Commons or the legal realist Robert Hale, remained marginalized.²⁸ The latter detailed the inner operation of legal institutions and their impact on power, subordination, and inequality, but this had little impact on the prevailing ideology that law was neutral. The mantra of law's neutrality was revived after World War II after overt references to fascism were deleted from the relevant codifications in countries that had embraced it, including Germany, Italy, and Japan. Against the backdrop of the Cold War and the expansion of socialism throughout the world, academics and politicians in the West sought to legitimize law as a neutral form of social order. Even the literature on comparative capitalism paid scant attention to law.²⁹

Still, some theorists continued to inquire into the role of law in capitalism. An example is Nicos Poulantzas, a Greek legal theorist and student of the French philosopher Louis Althusser.³⁰ Not a fan of either capitalism or the real existing socialism, he developed a critique of capitalism and its law that builds on Marxist theory but also incorporates non-Marxist theories such as those of Michel Foucault. Capitalist law, he wrote, "forms an *axiomatic system*, comprising a set of *abstract, general, formal and strictly regulated norms.*"³¹ This form "is inextricably bound up with the real fracturing of the social body in the social division of labour."³² Far from offering spheres of autonomy and freedom for individuals against the state, as many liberals would assert, individual rights splinter society and, as a result, render it more, not less, governable by the state. The antithesis of public and private law that Pashukanis identified is present in Poulantzas's argument as well: "This law institutes individuals as juridico-political subjects-persons.... It consecrates ... the differential fragmentation of agents (individualization) by elaborating the code in which these differentiations are inscribed and on the basis of which they exist without calling into question the political unity of the social formation."[33]

A critical figure in this system is the jurist—"a man of the law who legislates, knows the laws and regulations, and applies them in concrete ways." By contrast, the masses are ignorant of the law and are kept ignorant. "[T]he law's secret is built into this law and juridical language itself," thereby ensuring that the masses "remain dependent upon, and subordinated to, state functionaries," to which one might add attorneys, whom I have labeled the "masters" of the code of capital.[34] Still, the greatest danger emanates from the state, which, according to Poulantzas, enjoys substantial autonomy over social forces because it controls "a monopoly of violence, and ultimately terror, *a monopoly of war.*"[35]

This position is remarkably close to that of liberal philosophers like Judith Shklar, who stressed the unique threat of state power in her "Liberalism of Fear."[36] In her view, the state's monopoly of violence makes the separation of a private sphere from the public sphere (and by extension of private and public law) essential and non-negotiable for a liberal because only by protecting private autonomy can individual freedom be realized. However, this does not mean that power is always coercive or necessarily vested in the state. As Poulantzas emphasized, in most societies overt state violence has decreased in inverse relation to the legitimizing power of law: "The State had to apply less force *to the very degree that* it holds a monopoly of its legitimate use."[37] Law facilitates the seemingly peaceful domination of some (the ruling class) over the rest, although the latter likely experience this as another form of violence.[38] As the struggle shifted to law, the contours of the state and of state-endorsed power, which Poulantzas likened to a topography that frames these struggles, became ever more blurred.[39]

Unlike the old institutionalists of the early twentieth century, including Thorstein Veblen and John Commons, for example, mainstream economists long ignored law or, rather, assumed rather than explained its role in structuring economic relations. This changed somewhat in the 1990s with the emergence of the field of "new institutional economics," which emphasized institutions as a critical ingredient for economic growth and development.[40] Soon law was identified as a promoter of economic and, in particular, of financial development.[41] The "new comparative economics" sought to explain differences among capitalist systems now that socialism had failed and the field of old comparative economics between socialism and capitalism was no longer relevant.[42] Reflecting the rise of financial capitalism in the late twentieth century, this new line of research explored the legal conditions for the development of financial markets.[43] Furnishing the correct law for finance became the state's most critical function. By contrast, big states that sought to govern the economy through labor law and other regulations were found to be obstacles to financial-market development.[44]

Interestingly, the new comparative economics located the origins of law not in economic conditions but in the *political* conditions that prevailed at the outset (the *legal origin*) when, according to these economists, the dominant legal systems—the common law and the civil law—were formed.[45] France is depicted as the paradigmatic example of the state exercising central control over the law. French rulers long struggled to assert control over a divided territory. Once they succeeded, according to this account, they centralized legal control and used it to entrench their power. England, by contrast, was pacified internally after the Norman Conquest. A relatively weak central ruler secured his control by leaving legal power in the hands of local elites, and this is said to have resulted in a much more decentralized legal system.

Leaving aside whether this account of the new comparative economics accurately depicts history, it illustrates some of the core assumptions about the law, the state, and the economy made by this school of thought. Following in the Keynesian tradition, this school places finance, not production or trade, center stage.[46] The main purpose of the law is to support investors in their pursuit of financial gain. The state is depicted as a product of political circumstances that rendered it with more or less centralized control over the economy. Rather than economic conditions shaping the state and its laws, as traditional Marxism would suggest, the economy emerges at the intersection of politics and law. Missing in this account is a recognition of the importance of historical contingencies. Even if institutions are path dependent, the idea that historical choices a millennium ago explain financial-market development today defies belief.[47]

In all these accounts, law is depicted as a product of the state, but what the state is and how it interacts with the law remain nebulous. Different conceptions of "the state" compete with one another, even within the same ideological camp, without advancing a comprehensive theory of the state. The state is at times depicted as an agent that empowers capital, which some celebrate and others denounce.[48] The importance of the state's willingness and capacity to guarantee private property rights and enforce contracts has become a staple in economic discourse, even in the face of empirical evidence that has demonstrated the importance of health, education, and other social provisioning for long-term economic success.[49] More fundamentally, the theory of the state that different camps espouse in debates about capitalism are often hidden behind metaphors of the state as neutral arbiter in liberal theories or as instrument of the ruling class in Marxist ones, both of which are oversimplistic.

Turning to political philosophy for a more nuanced account of the state and its role in capitalist regimes does not always help.

Philip Pettit, for example, derives the state from a hypothetical genealogy in his recent book.[50] Not class or social struggles, but the need to create structures that perform state-like functions explains the emergence of states, their endurance, and indeed their inevitability: "The genealogy starts from a prepolitical society of moderately self-regarding, moderately rational, and mutually dependent agents, operating under conditions of relative scarcity and an approximately equal balance of power."[51] Even more than the "legal origin" story of the new comparative economics, this model abstracts from historical circumstances to explain the emergence of a state that mediates among formally equal social actors. Contrast this with an account by the social historian Charles Tilly that is based on the history of state formation in early modern Europe.[52] Tilly likens state-making with war-making and organized crime. The state is the product of power struggles, and state structures emerge from attempts to appease different factions and win over their clients. Viewed in this light, the characteristics of the political community that Pettit identifies as the precursor to statehood are in fact the products of an often violent state-building process.[53]

The approach one adopts to explain the state matters a great deal in how one might understand the state in capitalism: an external force that enforces the rules of the game as a neutral arbiter, as Douglass North insisted, or a "condensation of the relations of forces," specifically of class struggles, and as such a product of these forces, as Poulantzas suggested.[54] In the latter account the state, through its various agents and offices, is the topography or space—physically in terms of territory and figuratively in terms of the terrain of power struggles—within which different constituencies, or social forces, vie for power and influence. It is neither static nor neutral, nor can it be, because the state's actions and policies are shaped by the struggles that its topography both enables and seeks to contain.

This picture of the state seems to contrast with the most common depiction of the modern Weberian state as a rational bureaucracy.[55] Yet Weber's own view was more nuanced. As Alan Scott noted, Weber predicted the bureaucratization of political and economic life, but at the same time emphasized power's "*diffusion* throughout social networks and relationships" in an almost Foucauldian sense of "capillary power" that "subvert[s] the lines of demarcation between state and society."[56] Thus, the critical question to ask about Weber's state theory, Scott suggests, is not *what* but *where* the state is. This question helps situate "the state" within multiple and interdependent social forces that constitute it and that define and constrain its ability to act as an autonomous agent. Poulantzas captured the predicament of the modern state as having been "*caught in its own trap*":

> The metaphor is not too strong: from now on, the State can go neither backwards nor forwards, can neither stand outside nor control the heart of the economy. At one and the same time, it is driven to do both too much (crisis-inducing intervention) and too little (being unable to affect the deep causes of the crises). The State is constantly oscillating between the two terms of the alternative: withdraw and/or get further involved. It is not an all-powerful State with which we are dealing, but rather a State with its back to the wall and its front poised before a ditch.[57]

Whether Poulantzas viewed the law as a trap that, like a spider's web, ensnarls the state and deprives it of the capacity to act autonomously, is not clear. In my view, such an interpretation would be not only plausible but compelling. Law both empowers and limits state action. It enables the state to reach deep into society, but it also empowers private actors to oppose or evade the state's reach without sacrificing the use of law to advance their own interests and shield them from the state. And when the state engages with private actors in the marketplace, the rules of this game, forged in private law, force the state to play on the terms that private actors have set.[58] If this diagnosis is correct, then the state is not autonomous from these social forces and calling for the state to free society from the excesses of capitalism is therefore misguided. Needed instead is a reconfiguration of the state's topography, which requires a realignment of private law and its normative foundations with principles of constitutional democracy—in short, the democratization of private law.

This perspective is deeply at odds with prevailing views among economists as well as legal scholars steeped in the tradition of law and economics. They view the economy as being separate from the state, and they rarely discuss relations of power.[59] To them, the economy is about the exchange of goods and services, which they imagine to take place on a level playing field that is populated by individuals who are formally equal and free to bargain with one another for mutually beneficial outcomes.[60] The ability of some to amass wealth is likely to be attributed to superior skills, not power or biases in the legal system that result in structural inequality. Most would acknowledge that property rights and contracts are critical for a market economy to function, to create incentives and facilitate binding commitments, but few are willing to concede law's role as constitutive for the economy, as this would imply that a different law might also instill a different economic order.

Nowhere is the agnosticism about power more apparent than in theories that explain property rights without accounting for their origins or function as stabilizers of hierarchical relations of power. The famous Coase theorem is often cited in support of the proposition that the original allocation of property rights is irrelevant because actors can reallocate these rights to achieve the efficient allocation of goods and resources.[61] Transaction costs, not inequality, are the major impediment, and efficiency, not equity, is the goal. Social inequities are said to be best addressed ex post by the state, which may redistribute some wealth with the help of taxation, and not by altering the private-law institutions that channel the allocation of goods.[62]

Yet property is never just control over an object; it is always about the relations to others with respect to it.[63] The disregard of this relational, or social, aspect of property is deeply ingrained in economic thinking and is also reflected in capitalist law. Control over and benefits from an asset are placed in the hands of a single owner, who may act as a quasi-autocrat irrespective of the effects this might have on non-owners or the asset. Capitalist ownership is about maximizing pecuniary gain from an asset—about enclosure, coding, and exhaustion—not preservation or care. It should therefore not come as a surprise that the most powerful owners in capitalist economies are not individuals in pursuit of freedom or happiness, but business corporations whose primary purpose is the maximization of profits for their investors, no matter what the costs to labor, communities, or the environment.

Corporations are large bureaucratic structures with centralized management that administer production and seek to control the costs of inputs, including supplies and labor. They look more like states than humans, and, like states, they are legal, not natural, persons with a potentially infinite life span. Their very existence poses problems for economic theories that idealize the market as the most efficient way for organizing economic relations. Were this the case, Ronald Coase famously asked, why would firms even exist at all?[64] The answer he gave is revealing, and perhaps more supportive of Marxist accounts than he would have admitted. Firms exist because they replace horizontal relations in markets with authority. The owner of the firm can hire and fire labor and dictate the firm's internal relations. Oliver Hart and John Moore even developed a formal model to arrive at Marx's insight that the ownership of the means of production is the source of power over labor.[65] Not markets, but hierarchies, dominate capitalist economies, and they rule not just by price but by law and fiat. They write their own labor and consumer contracts, and for their internal affairs prefer autocratic over participatory governance.

Capitalism came first, and democracy only later, as Jonathan Levy noted in his account of the ages of American capitalism.[66] The promises of constitutional democracy were curtailed at the outset, because constitutional democracies failed to infuse capitalism with the same normative principles that animate them: collective self-determination and accountability of power wielders to their subjects. Instead, the private law that enabled capitalism was incorporated wholesale into this new order and offered additional protection by enshrining individual rights, including the right to property, in it. This set the stage for the duality of law that Pashukanis identified as the essence of capitalist law: public and private, collective and individual. Private law empowered private actors to reverse the gains that democracies made on behalf of the weakest parts of society by giving them the legal tools to build out their own power through law, to use law to shield themselves from state control, and to control others. A powerful example is the repurposing of the Fourteenth Amendment to the U.S. Constitution, which was adopted after the Civil War to protect the property rights of former slaves. It prohibits depriving *any person* of "life, liberty, or property" without "due process of Law" and tasks federal courts with enforcing these rights because the drafters apparently did not trust state courts to do so. Instead of advancing the interests of the Black population, however, the Fourteenth Amendment was turned into an instrument that expanded the property rights of corporations.[67] As Supreme Court Justice Hugo Black noted in a dissent in 1938, "less than one-half of 1 percent [of all cases] invoked it [the Fourteenth Amendment] in protection of the Negro race, and more than 50 percent asked that its benefits be extended to corporations."[68]

This book is part of a broader conversation in the legal academy about bringing power and political economy back into the analysis of law. It seeks to correct a long-term trend within the economic analysis of law: a focus on efficiency, with less attention to how law constitutes relations of social and political power. To date, the new "law and political economy" (LPE) project that was launched in 2017 has been an open tent. Its founders intended to create the space for deliberation about legal education and scholarship.[69] LPE is not the first attempt to do that, but follows in the steps of legal realism in the first half of the twentieth century and critical legal studies in the latter. What exactly LPE might add and whether it should depart from or instead reinvigorate these earlier debates is warmly contested among scholars who sympathize with this new movement.

On one side of this debate, Samuel Moyn has called for a renewed engagement with critical legal studies, with a focus on Roberto Unger's work.[70] Moyn argues for a general social theory of how law works, a theory that recognizes the use of law as a tool for domination and exploitation, as well as its potential for change. "No credible theory of law could omit the situated freedom of agents to alter the terms of their domination—even, in rare instances, to lift it," he writes.[71] The capacity to imagine an alternative world that does not dispense with but embraces law as the representation of an alternative is core to his argument. The freedom of different agents to transform the terms of their social and personal lives may vary, and may indeed be constrained by law, but "there is always freedom under domination."[72] Law is never fully deterministic, but always leaves room for alternatives. In fact, one does not have to choose between radical indeterminacy on one hand and crude functionalism on the other. There is room for "relative autonomy" of action, and this autonomy can be found by "theorizing how ideological work in interpretation shapes and stabilizes social order"—or, one might add, destabilizes it.[73]

On the other side of the debate, Jeremy Kessler opposes the revival of critical legal studies and instead proposes the adoption of a minimal historical materialist account of law (MHMAL).[74] Kessler agrees with Moyn that LPE needs a social theory of law, but following the Marxist tradition, he suggests that such a theory should take account of the materialist conditions for legal orders. He posits three principles of MHMAL: First, "social reality at a given place and time is ultimately determined by the development of the productive forces at that place and time." Second, "the relations of production tend to develop in a manner that is favorable to the use of the productive forces for the continued production and reproduction of human life." And third, "[j]ust as the relations of production are functionally explained by, while being essential to, the production of the productive forces, the other social relations—legal, political, religious, familial, artistic, etc.—tend to develop in a manner that is conducive to the stabilization and reproduction of the social relations of production."[75] In effect, Kessler holds that ideas and imagination are not a sufficient basis for a social theory of law. The materialist foundations leave a direct imprint in the law because the law tends to lag behind materialist conditions and oftentimes reflects what was rather than what is or could be. For this reason, he rejects a simplistic determinism between the material conditions that bring law about and the context in which it is applied, which is also why he labels his approach "minimalist materialist."

My own analysis of capitalism as a legal regime can be situated somewhere in between these two positions, but closer to Kessler than Moyn. My starting point is that, as Poulantzas has pointed out, the attempt to develop a general theory of law (or the state) is ultimately futile. It is more useful to consider a theory of the prevailing regime—that is, of capitalist law—and explain the conditions under which it emerged, evolved, or might be transformed. One may, of course, imagine a different order that is divorced from its materialist conditions, and it may be important to develop such a utopia in order to create the momentum for real change. However, without adequate consideration of the actually existing conditions of capitalism, such a theory is bound to remain utopian. Moyn, following Unger, may be right that there is always freedom underneath domination, but if a social theory of law is meant to offer the prospect of actual change, it must point to the mechanisms by which the dominant system has been able to rule for so long and reconstitute itself time and again despite attempts to open it up to alternative visions. In large measure, I argue, these mechanisms can be found in the law, which is why the transformation of law is critical for moving beyond capitalism.

This latter point also sets me apart from Kessler. I sympathize with his call for closer attention to the material conditions of economic power, but my position differs from MHMAL in one important respect: In my view, law is foundational for the production and reproduction of capital, the asset, and of capitalism, the regime. Law might even be described as a productive force in its own right, because it is the means that allows holders of assets to extract their pecuniary value. This is most apparent when considering the creation of entirely new asset classes in law with the help of intellectual-property rights, for example, the legal engineering of financial products, or the capture and exploitation of data for profit. Patents, financial products, and even data as an asset distinct from the persons that generate it, exist only by virtue of the law. This makes it impossible to draw a clear line between (physical) power on the one hand and a right (or legal entitlement) on the other, as G. A. Cohen and Kessler after him have proposed.[76] The assets owe their existence to the law, not to a physical force; their holders owe the assets themselves and the power that flows from them entirely to the law. Even for tangible assets, the scope of power they confer on their owners is rooted in the law; property owners may physically control their land with the help of fences or weapons, but they cannot sell or mortgage it without legal title. And the business corporation, which has become a dominant force in capitalist systems of all stripes, shows that law not only reflects but also transforms the materialist base into one that may be socially constructed but is quite capable of reproducing itself without the need for a material base. Witness only the proliferation of legally incorporated investment vehicles in search of expected future returns or the rise of cryptocurrencies. No doubt, economic interests played a role in shaping the law that is the source code for these assets, but, conversely, the law also created the opportunity for powerful economic forces to emerge, entrench, and enrich themselves.

Human beings have the capacity to organize their social relations with reference to abstract norms and generalizable conventions, which, because of their abstract nature, can be used in many different ways and put to very different ends than those intended by the original lawmaker. Capitalism emerged at a time when a highly unequal distribution of resources coincided with a legal evolution that embraced abstract concepts of law that could be applied irrespective of context and thus abstracted from the materialist conditions. Capitalism, I would argue, is so powerful and so difficult to overcome because it relies not only, and no longer even primarily, on natural resources but also on social resources, including the legal and monetary systems. Controlling these resources is ultimately more important than controlling the material objects that are coded as capital.

Arguing that capitalism is a legal regime acknowledges the capacity of societies to create immaterial resources, such as legal and monetary systems, and extend them in space (from a community to a state to the global system) and in time (from the past to the present and, critically for capitalism, from the future to the present). This does not mean that humans can escape the constraints of materialism—in particular, of the naturally bounded planet Earth they inhabit. But it helps explain why capitalism and its beneficiaries will not easily succumb to these natural constraints. After centuries of relentless expansion, the expectation still is that further expansion is possible. Expansion is necessary for the survival of capitalism, which puts it on a collision course with nature. This raises the question of whether there is an exit from this system and how the system might be transformed. Traditionally, Marxists have called for revolution, a violent overthrowing of the ruling class. This has never happened in advanced capitalist countries, seems unlikely, and is also undesirable. As an alternative, countries have experimented with social welfarism and attempts to constrain capitalism with the help of public law and regulation. The success of this reform agenda has often been only temporary because access to private law made it fairly easy to circumvent the constraints that public law imposed on capital. What is needed is therefore a transformation of the system. Poulantzas likened the path toward a different future to "walking on a tight-rope."[77] This metaphor rules out cutting the rope in the hope that an alternative regime might emerge spontaneously from the crash. One must stay on the rope to ensure that the "state economic apparatus *as a whole*" will be transformed, which will happen only "*in stages.*"[78]

3

Legal Empowerment

Power is inherent in all social relations. It cannot be abolished or wished away; instead, it must be channeled into forms in which it can be checked and held to account. The concept of power has a long and contested history.[1] For the purpose of this analysis, I start with the most basic definition—namely, the capacity to make others do what they would not themselves choose to do.[2] These choices may be nudged or coerced, or be the product of peer pressure, network effects, misinformation, or even fraud. Any external pressure that drives choices toward the power wielder's rather than the actor's preferred outcome is a product of power rather than free choice.[3]

Legally sanctioned power is deeply woven into the fabric of modern societies. It is backed by the centralized means of coercion, which in turn are controlled by the checks and balances found in modern constitutions and by the social norms that determine support for the use of this power, but also by the capacity of individual actors to employ legal power to their own ends. To appreciate the power of law in structuring socioeconomic relations in capitalist regimes, one cannot merely ask why people obey the law.[4] Instead, one must interrogate why some may legitimately claim to have the law on their side and others don't, and what forces determine whether the weak or the strong come out of this struggle as winners.

The modules of the code of capital enable resourceful actors to fashion their own interests as legal claims and to claim law's authority to enforce those claims against others. The origins of these claims lie in Roman private law, which conferred on actors that claimed to have the law on their side the right to invoke state power *against* others.⁵ For private actors to take the law into their own hands, the legal claims must be relatively freestanding, unmoored from the social context in which they first arose, which may otherwise constrain their use or the ability to repurpose them. In short, it must become possible to instrumentalize the legal claim without compromising its authority.

The German legal sociologist Max Weber described the evolution of law from the Middle Ages to modern times using the debt contract as his example. Debt morphed from a socially embedded relation of mutually owed obligations into a "pure" purpose contract (*Zweckvertrag*).⁶ It became transferable and, in the hands of creditors, evolved into a financial asset that today is issued and traded simply for profit. Relations of debt evolved from mutual obligations into an instrumentality of private power that creditors can wield over debtors with the law on their side. It is no coincidence that in the second half of the nineteenth century the law began to strengthen the rights of creditors even at the expense of property owners.⁷ Creditors were empowered to seize assets, including eventually land and mansions, to satisfy their claims. Their reach was limited only later by some debtor protections built into more recent bankruptcy codes that safeguard debtors' most essential goods from seizure. Not surprisingly, it was exactly at this time that agricultural land lost its position as the most important source of private wealth to financial instruments.⁸ In short, although debt has been part and parcel of socioeconomic relations for millennia, its nature changed with the evolution of capitalism.⁹

The transformation of law affected not only the objects of transactions, such as land or debt, but also their subjects. The law that evolved in the West in modern times (since the rediscovery of Roman law in the thirteenth century) organizes social life around a legal subject, the objects and claims that it can legally control, and the ways in which control can be exercised in relation to others. Put in less abstract terms, the law determines who can own and contract, what can be owned or controlled by other means, and the extent to which others are prevented from accessing or sharing control rights. This body of law is called "private law" because its main function is to govern relations between legal subjects, not between them and the state. Consent, not coercion, is the primary governance tool, and a breach of contract or an infringement of property rights is considered a violation of the law. The law assumes that private actors are formally equal, that consent is given voluntarily, that rights are antecedent to transactions rather than their product, and that by threatening to punish infringements of rights ex post, the law deters violations ex ante.

All three assumptions are problematic. Steep differences in resource endowments question the ideals of an economy in which all can participate on equal terms and the price mechanism will achieve outcomes that may not only be efficient but also just.[10] These material differences have been augmented by structural differences in access to the law, its making, its interpretation, and its enforcement.[11] Only few can afford to hire the legal skills that might allow them to strike a better deal or to avoid regulatory costs or taxes and in this way create a comparative advantage relative to everyone else who plays by the rules. Moreover, private law structures the position of legal subjects in ways that affect their ex ante bargaining positions. There is no "veil of ignorance" in the Rawlsian sense that prevents legal subjects from exploiting their positions relative to others, as these positions are known to both parties.[12] On the contrary, strategic actors carefully weigh every option to ensure that they will get the upper hand in a given transaction and, even more importantly, in future cases. This is why they litigate the same issue not just once but repeatedly, carefully selecting cases that could assure them a new precedent or the overturning of an existing one. As Marc Galanter put it, those who can afford to be repeat players play not just for the outcome but for the rules that help determine future outcomes.¹³ Private law does not just deter, it empowers sophisticated parties to use it for creating new rights by recombining existing law and extending its use to new asset frontiers. As Gary Becker pointed out, deterrence is a function of the probability of being caught and the penalty one might face.¹⁴ This logic works not only for criminal law but also for private law: Actors who do not have to face legal challenges but can instead threaten others with their transactional sophistication or litigation prowess are unlikely to be deterred by the threat of litigation by less resourceful parties. In short, the law does not reside outside social relations; it shapes them from the inside. It is also shaped by them, because the power relations that law helps create also color the future development of the law.

The quintessentially hierarchical institution of private law is property rights. The title holder gets to decide how to use an object and to tell others what to do or not to do with it as well.¹⁵ Property rights empower owners to rule over others by right, not just by might. The ideational roots of individual rights within this arrangement can be traced to early modern times when the individual replaced the family, clan, and guild as the central unit of social organization. Not one's social status as peasant, aristocrat, or clergy but individual rights qua legal subject became the linchpin for legal empowerment.¹⁶

Individual rights that are protected by law are powerful because they create a sphere of autonomy for the human being against others and against an overburdening state. This idea of individual rights found its way into the French Declaration of the Rights of Man and of the Citizen (1789), the U.S. Bill of Rights (1791), and later into the constitutions of many countries as well as international conventions.¹⁷ In private law, the notion of individual (or subjective) rights has an even longer history. Roman law recognized the concept of individualized "absolute" property rights, or rights *in rem*, an idea that deeply influenced the evolution of property law in modern Europe and spurred the development of capitalism.[18] As Marx and Engels argued, owning the means of production allows capitalists to extract surplus from labor, an idea that economic models have more recently confirmed.[19]

Originally, property rights were about physical objects, as reflected in the core property rights to use, possess, and alienate an object, but this idea has been carried much further. Intangibles have become objects of statutory property rights that stipulate the conditions for patents, trademarks, or copyrights. Human behavior too has become the stuff of ownership—not for the behavior-emitting producers of data but for actors that control the technology to grab their data and put it on a device.[20] The most recent frontier is artificial intelligence (AI), which is threatening to displace writers as creators and vest the power to create and be recognized as a creator in the digital coders that control the algorithms and in their financiers.[21]

Although individual property rights are central features of capitalism and capitalist law, for much of human history, land, water, air, and other resources were held in common and governed by communal norms. Societies did not simply succumb to the "tragedy of the commons"; they found ways to govern such resources collectively and quite successfully.[22] In fact, it is a deep irony of history that the age of individual property rights has produced the greatest tragedy of the commons—climate change—which threatens the survival of humans on this planet. Contrary to standard economic theory, property rights did not ensure that property owners internalized the costs of using their property.[23] In capitalist systems, property rights were configured as a license to externalize these costs to others—to society and the environment. This follows directly from property as a presumption of a right to do as one pleases until challenged—the burden falling on the challenger. Moreover, shareholders in corporations are protected from liability for damages resulting from the conduct of the companies they own. They may lose their individual investment, but they will never pay for the damages to others that the profit-seeking corporations they invest in cause. In addition, many states adopted statutes that set liability ceilings for risky undertakings, like operating railways or a nuclear power plant, limiting the liability of the corporation itself for causing harm in pursuit of these activities.[24]

Roman property law was premised on three types of goods: private goods, common goods, and goods that belonged to no one, such as wild animals, which were up for grabs by taking possession of them.[25] By contrast, modern property rights start from the rights holder rather than the object. They are framed as abstract rights to an object, promise, or idea that are vested within someone, and this allows the rights holder—a natural or legal person—to rule over his property and exclude others. Because of their general and abstract nature, property rights are not limited to the specific objects or types of property for which they were first created, such as land or chattel.[26] Rather, property rights can be adapted to new resources that have the potential to create wealth for those who claim such resources as theirs. Under capitalist law, anything that can be owned may be and, as the history of capitalism suggests, eventually will be. Most legal systems today recognize property rights not only in tangible assets (such as land, houses, or objects like cars or machines) but also in intangibles or immaterial property, such ideas or inventions (patents) or words or brushstrokes put on paper (copyrights), as well as financial assets. "Things" as ephemeral as information and communication are owned by Big Tech companies, which capture them as if they were wild animals and place them behind technical and legal shields.[27] Even the air we breathe and the remaining spots of unspoiled nature are being turned into assets that can be owned and traded, allegedly to offset the damage that humans inflict on nature but without proof that this works.[28]

Although widely celebrated as the source of individual freedom, property rights are Janus-faced. They enhance the freedom of one by vesting him with power over others.[29] This relational aspect of property rights is often neglected in theories that focus on property as freedom primarily against the state but ignore the powers that flow from it and that can be used against others.[30] In capitalist regimes, property has become a critical module for coding priority rights that give the holder stronger rights relative to others: the right to exclude others from accessing an asset or resource, or the ability to seize an asset that has been collateralized ahead of other creditors.

In theory, the property rights of one person find their limitations in the rights of others.[31] In this view, property is a social relation, and its special status in the law, especially in relation to non-owners, must be justified.[32] Some aspects of property law do reflect the idea that property is not only for the rich and powerful, even in capitalist economies. These include marital properties or mandatory licenses for intellectual-property rights to enhance access to critical medicines, for example.[33] Still, the gist of property law in capitalist regimes has taken a different path and has empowered private actors, including corporations, to employ their assets to maximize profits and exert control over others they need for this endeavor. Entrepreneurs and businesses have frequently used property rights to challenge the rights of others, including collective labor rights the legislature sought to protect. The U.S. Supreme Court, for example, struck down a California law that gave labor unions access to agricultural employers' premises in order to meet with workers. This, the Supreme Court argued, was not merely a regulatory taking but outright expropriation—a "per se physical taking, requiring just compensation under the Takings Clause."[34] Not every court in every country will go that far. By comparison, the German constitutional court held that mandating equal representation of workers on the boards of private corporations was constitutional.[35] The constitutional framing of property rights can make an important difference. Whereas the U.S. Constitution protects individual property rights without further definition or determination about who has the power to determine their content, the German Basic Law provides that the limits and scope of property rights shall be defined by the legislature.[36] This suggests that the more abstract the concept and the less said in a statute or the constitution about who other than the courts might define property rights, the greater the powers of the courts and those who have access to them.

Vesting courts with the power to recognize new property rights or strike down legal restrictions on their use as expropriation has fueled the proliferation of property rights. In this sense, economic might, understood as access to lawyers with superior legal-coding strategies that help fashion economic interests as legally protected, makes right.[37] In this way, ownership, which was originally understood as a "use right" with respect to real or tangible objects, evolved into an option to turn any object, promise, or idea into a property right by demonstrating that pecuniary value could be extracted from it. Conversely, resources that cannot or should not be monetized are often denied property-rights protection. Indigenous peoples, for example, were long denied legal protection of their land-use rights because they refused to turn their land into a commodity that could be exploited by extracting its resources or exhausting its nutrients. Only in recent decades have some courts ruled otherwise and recognized as property rights their collective-use rights geared toward preserving, not exploiting, the land.[38]

The proliferation of private property rights and the ways in which they were molded by attorneys for their clients has altered the core tenets of property law, including the enumeration principle, which holds that property rights are limited to items that the law (not an asset holder) privileges as property.[39] In reality, new property rights are continuously created, sometimes by legislation or case law but more frequently by transposing in private transactions the abstract features of property rights to new assets. Today, we take it for granted that financial claims, which are contractual in nature, have been "assetized" or turned into quasi-objects that can be owned and traded.[40] Shareholders of corporations were long understood to be members of an organization before the idea that they were the owners of the firm took hold, with the further implication that their interests should trump the interests of all other corporate constituencies, including creditors and, of course, labor.[41]

Ownership status has become associated with the ability to extract profits from an asset, not just use value or affection. According to American jurisprudence on data ownership, the individuals who produce data on digital platforms don't own that information, because the information has no pecuniary value to them.[42] Only aggregate pools of data that have been cleansed and organized so that monetary value can be extracted can be owned. No matter that this line of reasoning runs roughshod over Locke's idea of ownership *through* labor (unless one discounts the labor of the data producer and values only the cleansing and organization done by the data harvester); it also turns on its head Marx's argument that ownership is the source of surplus extraction. In this rendering, by contrast, surplus extraction becomes the source of and the only justification for the legal protection of property rights.

The logical conclusion is that in capitalist law, whoever creates pecuniary value with something can claim ownership; and, conversely, whoever fails to extract value from things is in danger of losing title in favor of those that will.[43] As Marietta Auer explains: "Once intangibles were recognized as property, the forces of a legal order steeped in the ideas of the Enlightenment (*Vernunftrecht*), according to which the powers that come with property rights are justified whenever scarce resources can be turned into usable ones only through work or by taking possession of them, automatically push toward the further propertization of individual autonomy."[44] Indeed, these forces continue to create powerful incentives to induce conditions of scarcity as the lever for claiming rights not only to things but also over others.

When property rights are configured to empower the holders of assets to use those assets as they see fit, a collision between owners, each claiming a legal right to use their assets without interference by others, becomes inevitable. Although in relation to weaker rights, such as contractual rights, property rights can help establish priority without the need for litigation, priority rights are of little help when two claims of similar rank collide. Examining cases of this kind promises to reveal the normative bias of a seemingly neutral legal system.

The dispute between two farmers immortalized by the Coase theorem is a good starting point. The theorem states that in the absence of transaction costs, two parties with conflicting rights will bargain for an efficient outcome—provided that property rights were clearly, even if not efficiently, allocated.[45] In Coase's famous example, the cattle of one farmer destroy the crops of another farmer. Absent transaction costs, the two owners should solve this problem by calculating the costs and benefits their rights would bring in the absence of this collision and for the party with the greater benefits to compensate the other. A possible solution would be to build a wall and apportion its costs between the two; in the alternative, one farmer could acquire the other's land, or they could both opt for either cattle raising or crop farming. For arriving at an efficient outcome, the specific solution itself is less important than the fact that the parties trade their respective rights in pursuit of a mutually beneficial solution.

Still, even when one assumes that transaction costs are absent or kept under control, it does not follow that both parties would choose to bargain for what is best for both.[46] The cattle owner could simply ignore the crop farmer and allow his cattle to eat the crops, thus forcing his neighbor to either yield or sue. This alone places a heavy burden on the crop farmer because he is likely to bear at least some litigation costs.[47] Moreover, when similar rights collide, the outcome of a dispute is often uncertain. Whoever causes the damage has strong incentives to gamble on convincing a court that his right to impose damages on others ought to be protected. Cows, the farmer might argue, produce greater value for society than crops. Even if he does not win the case, he might have the resources to appeal or to relitigate. This is indeed how many disputed property rights have been eventually resolved in favor of the party with greater resources.

Take the *Sanderson* case, a prolonged legal dispute between Mr. and Mrs. Sanderson on the one hand and the Pennsylvania Coal Company on the other. In 1868, the Sandersons purchased a plot of land along Meadow Brook in Scranton, Pennsylvania. They built a home on the land, added a dam for fish and an ice pond, and used the brook's fresh water for an irrigation system, a fountain, and a cistern. In 1870, the Pennsylvania Coal Company started to mine two miles upstream from the Sandersons' property. Coal mining sets free acidic groundwater, which the company emptied into Meadow Brook, which flowed to the Sanderson's property—killing the fish, corroding the irrigation pipes, and making the water unfit for consumption.[48]

The Sandersons sued for damages. The first judge dismissed the case outright, concluding that there was loss but no injury (*damnum absque injuria*). Discharging acid water, the court reasoned, was a byproduct of coal mining, and Scranton was in a coal-mining state, which made these discharges highly predictable. In short, the Sandersons should have known that their property was impaired when they acquired it. The court of appeals reversed, concluding that the coal company's use of its own property did not justify inflicting injury on its neighbors' property.[49] The appeals court awarded $250 to the Sandersons, or a little less than $6,000 in 2024 dollars. This was only a fraction of what the Sandersons believed they were owed in light of the actual damages they had suffered, and so they brought their grievance to a different court, where a jury awarded them $2,872.74 in damages (over $67,000 today). The coal company struck back and appealed to the Pennsylvania Supreme Court. There, the company finally found open ears for an argument it had tried to advance all along—namely, that the *social interests* in coal mining should prevail over the rights of individual landowners like the Sandersons. If every landowner along a river could stop upstream industry, the company argued, economic progress would become impossible. The Pennsylvania Coal Company was developing the "great natural resources of a country" and should be allowed to proceed, even if this imposed costs on others. The court agreed. It ruled that the "necessities of a great community" were superior to the plaintiffs' individual property rights, which were downgraded to "a mere personal inconvenience."[50]

It is worth noting that the Sandersons did not try to stop the operations of the coal company altogether; all they sought was compensation for the damages they had suffered. This already marked a retreat from traditional nuisance law, which gave owners a veto right against any infringement of their property rights by others. U.S. courts increasingly turned this veto right into a right for compensation, or into compensation for what has been aptly called "judicially sanctioned private takings."[51] Paying compensation allowed resourceful corporations to grease the wheels of economic development by paying what was often little more than a token for violating others' property rights.

Courts in England stuck to the veto rule much longer. The sanctity of property rights was interpreted by the courts as a shield against *judicial* power as well.[52] As one chancellor noted, "[t]he Court has always protested against the notion that it ought to allow a wrong to continue simply because the wrongdoer is able and willing to pay for the injury he may inflict."[53]

Not the courts but Parliament should take the lead in determining how colliding property rights should be resolved. Still, English courts ultimately succumbed to the pressure of powerful litigants and "appropriate[d] for themselves a power unavailable at common law to award damages for future loss in lieu of an injunction."[54] By denying some owners the right to prevent actions that would predictably damage their property and forcing them to settle for compensation instead, the courts sanctioned private takings.

The choice of remedies when property rights collide has profound implications for the allocation of power and wealth in society. In a seminal paper, Guido Calabresi and Douglas Melamed explained that "society" not only must decide what entitlements (defined as any interest protected by law, such as property) to grant and "whom to entitle"—that is, how to allocate these entitlements. Society must also determine the second-order rules on how to protect these entitlements. In the absence of rules of this kind, it is impossible to solve conflicts between two or more equal rights, and as a result, the old principle "might makes right" would prevail.[55]

Calabresi and Melamed offered a simple typology of rules for solving conflicts between equal rights: a *property rule* to veto any intrusion; a *liability rule* that converts the veto right into money payments for damages; and *an inalienability rule* that prohibits the violation of interests altogether.[56] Even if the only goals a society pursues are efficiency and a (fairly) equitable distribution of costs and benefits, making the right call on these rules, they suggested, is complicated and requires not only technical acumen but moral judgment as well. Many trade-offs and judgment calls have to be made; some of them might later turn out to have been wrong yet will be difficult to reverse.

Importantly, the two authors showed that the liability rule, which courts have preferred because it makes virtually any conflict resolvable without favoring only one side, is at best an imperfect alternative to the property (or veto) rule. The former may grease the wheels and, in this way, help overcome hold-up problems. Converting all property into liability rules, however, would undermine the sanctity of property. This, they suggested, is why the penalties criminal law imposed on thieves exceeds the economic value of their bounty. After all, why bother to ask before taking something if the only penalty one faces is paying for it should one get caught?

Calabresi and Melamed also emphasized that bargaining and exchange between rights holders will not always produce results that are consistent with social goals.[57] Writing in 1972, they suggested that the inalienability rule, which prohibits bargains and imposes binding constraints, would be the right choice to protect future generations from the costs of environmental harm that society may be "powerless to reverse." This advice was not heeded. Inalienability rules, even in their softer version as environmental regulations that impose some restrictions on polluters but very little outright prohibition, were opposed by industry, which fought them tooth and nail, mostly through litigation and the lobbying of regulators and legislatures.

Many polluters have been able to avoid liability by employing the corporate form, which affords liability protection to shareholders, even when the shareholder is the parent company with 100 percent control. This has allowed corporations to employ their subsidiaries to inflict damage on others and the environment while shareholders of the parent company reap profits from these activities and escape liability. Only in recent years have some litigants been able to hold the parent company liable for damages that one of its subsidiaries inflicted on others. A prominent example is litigation against Shell in the United Kingdom and the Netherlands by fishermen in Nigeria whose fishing grounds were destroyed by pollution. It took thirteen years for a Dutch court to rule on the matter. Only in December 2022, more than fifteen years after the action had been brought, did Shell finally pay 15 million euros to the victims.⁵⁸ Liability of the parent company was also confirmed in a parallel case in the United Kingdom through the court's use of a simple, centuries-old legal principle: the duty of care. Under agency law, the court ruled, the principal is liable for torts committed by an agent that the principal controls.⁵⁹ At least implicitly, this ruling questions the doctrine of "piercing the corporate veil," which has long protected parent companies and other shareholders from liability because courts have insisted that the legal veil between two corporate entities must be protected and can be pierced only if the parent company has used its subsidiary like a plaything or inflicted injustice on others.⁶⁰ The argument used in the "duty of care" case against Shell is a powerful example of how existing law offers a well of arguments and doctrines that could be employed against capital.

Property rights structure the relations between owners and between owners and non-owners, but in doing so, they also structure social relations. Changes in property rights affect and can transform social relations without reverting to (overt) violence. This tends to work better when the rights of the weak, not the strong, are sacrificed, which has been the historical pattern, as suggested by empirical findings that the strength of property rights held by minorities is inversely related to economic growth.⁶¹ This stands in marked contrast to the positive correlation between property rights and growth rates that most econometric studies have established.⁶² These studies ignored how property rights were created in the first place, and at whose expense.⁶³ In fact, land reforms reallocating land from the powerful to the poor have been rare, notwithstanding empirical data suggesting that such a reallocation would be economically beneficial.⁶⁴ Often those reallocations succeeded only under the pressure of outside forces, such as an occupying power, as in postwar Japan, where the American occupational forces motivated land reforms not on economic efficiency grounds but with the goal of deepening democracy in Japan.⁶⁵

Another instructive case for understanding the societal dimensions of property rights is India. After over two centuries of colonial rule, first by the English East India Corporation and later by the Crown, the country finally achieved independence in 1947 and adopted its constitution in 1950.⁶⁶ One of the constitution's most controversial provisions was Article 31, which protected property as a fundamental individual right—an interesting choice for a country that sought to embark on a development process that would lift the majority of its population out of poverty. Many Indian politicians argued at the time that the strong protection of property rights would make it impossible to leave behind colonial structures, which had favored landlords over peasants and had become entrenched as English colonial rule protected the landlord's property rights.⁶⁷ Article 31 offered the standard protection of property rights as negative rights against the state: "No person shall be deprived of his property save by authority of the law." It mandated compensation, but without requiring that such compensation be "just" or in line with "market value." Most importantly, Article 31 ruled out judicial review of the compensation paid.

That did not prevent landowners from trying to challenge land reform anyhow by mobilizing the constitution's equal protection clause—invoking the powerful argument of formal equality. Although the Supreme Court of India ultimately rejected this argument, several lower courts ruled in their favor. For fear of further attacks on the reform agenda, the Indian Parliament amended Article 31 in 1951 and again in 1964 to specify that legislative takings could not be voided by the courts. In addition, a "constitutional vault" removed a list of laws from judicial review altogether. The battle did not end there, but eventually Article 31 was replaced by a new provision, Article 300, which downgraded property from a fundamental right to a simple right. At face value, this appears to have been a win for opponents of private property rights, but it ended up strengthening the powers of owners because it also stripped away the immunity from judicial review that Article 31 had enshrined.[68]

The battle over property rights in India has been widely interpreted as a clash between the legislature and the judiciary in which the judiciary undermined sweeping socialist reforms by upholding the property rights of the few. Rashmi Venkatesan paints a different picture that describes the legal contestation over property rights as part of a "passive revolution" that paved the way for capitalist modernity. The key question for India's political elite, she suggests, was how to "protect the right to property as a fundamental right in a way that allowed the post-colonial state to dismantle colonial property rights (especially zamindari [landowners'] rights) in order to hasten 'development.'"[69] Without overcoming the vestiges of feudalism and colonialism, development would be impossible. Weakening the property rights of entrenched landowners who were likely to block reforms (and indeed tried) was necessary in India, just as land reform in Japan was necessary to support economic structures that were better aligned with democratic values. In light of these cases, it is worth pondering the need for property reforms in the heartlands of capitalism—the United States and the United Kingdom, where property rights to financial assets have been consolidated in the hands of a small elite—to ensure the survival of democracy and foster broadly shared development.

Unlike India's constitution, the post-apartheid constitution of South Africa did not empower the legislature to engage in redistribution on a scale that would have made a difference to most people in the country. Inequality has increased rather than decreased since the end of apartheid, and the most valuable resources, including much of the arable land, have remained in the hands of a small elite, which is still predominantly, although no longer exclusively, white.[70] The South African Constitution of

1996 attempted to strike a different balance between protection of property rights and inclusive prosperity than India had struck. Its Article 25 protects and prohibits the arbitrary deprivation of property. To be lawful, expropriation must be based on a general law that provides for compensation, and the courts have the final say over the amount to be paid. The constitution's requirement that compensation be "just and equitable" and consider, among other factors, "the history of the acquisition and the use of property" had little effect in promoting the redistribution of land and natural resources.

True to the neoliberal paradigm, the reallocation of property rights in South Africa was not executed by way of a state-instigated land reform but through voluntary bargains. With the advice of the World Bank, the new government pursued a "willing seller—willing buyer" strategy, which left the decision to put up land for reallocation in the hands of the white propertied class and forced the government to pay the asking price lest it wished to engage in lengthy court battles.[71] Even members of the Black population that had been pushed off their land were not restituted but pacified with cash handouts instead of property rights. Finally, in 2008 the legislature introduced a bill allowing for expropriation *without* compensation, albeit under highly restrictive conditions. The law requires a public purpose for the expropriation and permits such expropriation only when the land has been left unused or is being employed primarily for speculative purposes (that is, is not being used for its core functions) or when an owner has abandoned the land.[72] After several failed attempts, the law finally passed in September 2022, only to be decried inside and outside the country for breaching the rule of law and threatening the sanctity of property rights.[73] Hardly anyone asked *whose* property rights were at stake or under what conditions they had acquired them, or whether social progress and economic development might not be better served by empowering more people with resources and rights.

Shifting the gaze from individual owners to the societal impact of property rights reveals the distributional effects of property rights and their tendency to deepen social cleavages. Property owners don't always spearhead economic progress or promote efficiency with salutary effects for the rest. They are just as likely to create gridlock and block progress.[74] In South Africa, for example, entrenched landowners successfully blocked a deep social transformation to benefit the country's majority Black population that apartheid had deprived of political and economic opportunities. Similarly, today, natural-resource companies stand in the way of an energy transition from brown (polluting) to green (sustainable), using every legal tool in their toolbox. They have lobbied against regulation; they have sued sovereign states that have announced plans to phase out coal or oil, claiming that these states are infringing their investments; and they have applauded politicians seeking to end the promotion of "environmental, social, and governance" (ESG) investing.[75] Some governments have fought back and have withdrawn from the Energy Charter Treaty, which empowers energy companies to sue governments of other countries in which they invested for infringing on their investments. This is an important, if belated, step in preventing powerful energy companies from holding hostage states that dare challenge their interests in the name of sustainable economic development.[76] Property rights legalize the control that owners can exert over a resource and their power to determine what others may or may not do in relation to it. Once property rights are recognized and formalized, few questions are asked about the genesis of these rights. Who had rights to the assets before formalization? Whose rights were extinguished? And how fair was the process by which assets were formalized? The legal vindication of legal property rights extinguishes questions like these along with the claims that preceded it.[77]

William Blackstone famously called property a "despotic dominion."[78] Although property rights are still a bedrock of capitalism, in its current iteration as financial and informational capitalism, one could argue that contracts have surpassed property as the primary mode for some to dominate the rest.[79] With the help of modern information technology, a single contract can be imposed on millions of people, thereby subjecting them to the will of the company that furnishes the contract. In this way, contractual rights are used to establish priority rights for the party with the stronger bargaining power relative to all its counterparties.

Digital platforms, including Facebook, Google, Amazon, and X, illustrate how contracts combined with network power (to use David Grewal's term) create a new type of "despotic dominion." When signing up for these platforms, each user accepts the same standardized contract, with only some adaptations to the law prevailing in the user's jurisdiction. The European Union, for example, has imposed a consent requirement for the harvesting of personal data. Almost everywhere, platform users now have to click "agree" before accessing a platform.[80] Most do, although few actually opt out of features that allow for the surveillance of their personal information. The company at the center of this vast network sets the terms of use, including its rights to harvest personal information from platform users. In short, contracts have become universalized in ways that previously only property rights were. The latter were deemed absolute and directed against the world, whereas contracts had been thought of as relational, as binding two parties on the basis of mutual agreement. This illusion is hard to defend in the digital age.

Opting out of these contracts means opting out of an entire social world because, apart from a few "click the box" conditions, the terms of these contracts are non-negotiable. In 2024, close to 70 percent of the world population used some mobile device to connect to the internet, and over five of the eight billion people living today have a social-media identity.[81] In theory, people still have a choice. There is more than one social-media platform and there are billions of websites that one might visit or not. In practice, powerful network effects bind users to a platform once they have made enough connections on it.[82]

The fact that contracts tend to bind the weaker party to the will of a stronger party is, of course, nothing new. It has been a core feature of labor contracts throughout history, which inspired Marx's analysis of the exploitation of labor through capital. The ownership of the means of production gives capital control over labor because it gives capital the power to set the terms for the contractual relation with labor. A lot has been achieved since the nineteenth century in improving labor relations, mostly by legislative intervention that strengthened the hands of labor, including through collective bargaining, workplace safety standards, the regulation of work hours per day, and the prohibition of child labor, to mention just a few. One of the most powerful ways for labor to improve its bargaining power was unionization. In the United States, unionization reached a high point of 35 percent of the labor force in the 1930s and again in the 1950s, but declined to 20 percent in the 1980s and stands at roughly 10 percent today.[83] By contrast, in France and Italy close to 100 percent of employees today are members of a union, and the average for developed countries that are members of the Organisation for Economic Co-operation and Development (OECD) is 31 percent.[84]

There are many reasons for the decline in union membership, and they vary by country. Reasons include the active resistance of employers who, in the United States in particular, have been able to marshal the legal system to undermine the power of unions. Some of unions' most powerful economic weapons—secondary strikes or boycotts—are considered violations of antitrust rules in the United States.[85] Moreover, independent contractors—the preferred status of gig workers in the eyes of the company using them—are excluded from the National Labor Relations Act's coverage; independent contractors are also barred from organizing as a union, as this would be deemed anticompetitive. As mentioned earlier, legislation granting unions access to an employer's premises to organize was struck down as unlawful expropriation.[86] These examples show how artfully employers have structured economic relations with the help of property law as well as contract law to avoid the leveling of the playing field, through legislative change, between them and those who work for them.

Some multinational corporations have not shied away from flagrantly breaking local collective-bargaining rules in the host countries where they do business in an attempt to break the power of labor. Tesla, the U.S. electric-vehicle manufacturer headed by Elon Musk, simply refused to enter into a collective labor agreement mandated by Swedish law.[87] The company does not have major manufacturing in the country, but does have several repair stations for servicing its vehicles. About 130 mechanics who worked at Tesla repair stations walked out in the fall of 2023 and as of this writing have not returned.[88] Several other Swedish unions called for solidarity strikes, and even the postal workers refused to deliver license plates to new Tesla car buyers. Tesla sued the postal agency and won.[89] The company also temporarily brought in mechanics from neighboring countries—a move that was facilitated by the European Union's commitment to the free movement of labor. For the Swedish unions, the strikes have become a matter of principle. Once a multinational corporation is allowed to break local labor law by ignoring it, others will follow. For Tesla, this is all about global capitalism, a system in which corporations, not labor, set the rules of the game.

The case illustrates the battle between different modes of capitalism. The literature on the varieties of capitalism characterizes Continental European and Scandinavian countries as "coordinated," and the United Kingdom and the United States as "liberal" market economies.[90] Strong arguments have been made that each of these systems is sticky and that they are therefore unlikely to converge into a single system, notwithstanding the powerful forces of global capital flows.[91] Still, the Tesla case signifies the power of multinational corporations that have the resources and a long time horizon to take on not just some unions but the legal systems of sovereign states. To repeat Galanter's observation, they are playing for the rules, not just the outcome in an individual case.[92]

Worker protection in Europe started to weaken long before Tesla arrived. Harbingers of this weakening were the global outsourcing of labor, temporary workers, and the expansion of "ghost" work. Foreign direct investment has often been celebrated as a transfer of capital from the more to the less developed economies and as a powerful impetus for restructuring the recipient economies.[93] There are several problems with this view. Foreign direct investors do not necessarily bring capital, but instead often source it locally. And in recent decades more capital has flown from the global South to the global North, rather than in the opposite direction as this thesis predicts.[94] Foreign direct investment is also directly, and negatively, correlated with labor protection: Lower labor standards in most countries in the global South attract corporations from the global North.[95] In a free-market economy, this arbitrage effect would, of course, quickly diminish because workers would move North, but that is not possible in a global economy in which states limit the movement of people even as they endorse the free movement of goods, services, and capital. An important exception to this rule is the European Union, which enshrined the free movement of people as one of the four freedoms—the free movement of goods, persons, services, and capital—in the Treaty of Rome.[96]

The European Union is one of the few transnational regimes that protect the free movement of labor. Still, language barriers and home biases impose strong de facto barriers. Moreover, relentless competition with the rest of the world has weakened the resolve to strengthen labor rights in its member states; the introduction and legal recognition of temporary work is an important feature of this trend. By shifting labor from indefinite contracts to fixed-term contracts and by employing temp agencies, corporations have been able to avoid the costs of full-time employees that social-welfare states thrust upon them. In addition, they weakened the power of labor unions, which is strongest when labor has indefinite contracts and when workers can be terminated only for cause, as in many European countries, not at will as in the United States.[97] Temporary workers as a share of total dependent employees in OECD member countries has reached 11 percent on average, and in the Netherlands, Chile, and Finland, exceeds 25 percent.[98]

Another strategy to get around labor-protection rules that has become popular in the so-called sharing economy is the reclassification of workers as independent, short-term contractors, even when companies use them repeatedly.[99] It allows companies to hire workers for a specific task but deny them social protections that are tied to employment relations. As independent contractors, they are literally on their own. The best-known examples are Uber drivers, but the phenomenon goes well beyond them. Mary Gray and Siddharth Suri have coined the term "ghost work" to describe the situation of workers who are scattered around the world, each bidding from their personal computers for a task, with payment reflecting competitive bidding in a global marketplace.[100] Amazon advertised its "Mechanical Turk" workers as an "on-demand workforce."[101] For employers, this is the best of all worlds. They pay only for what they need on a given day. Labor bears not only the costs of reproduction (as Marx pointed out) but also of scrambling for work to make ends meet, without the ability to organize with others.

In this chapter, I have shown how property rights and contracts operate as legal empowerment for private actors, but not equally for all. In theory, property rights confer powerful protection on owners who obtain priority rights, which they can enforce against the world. However, when property rights collide, priority is often given to the economically more powerful actor, and ironically, this is justified with the social benefits they create by promoting development even as they pollute and destroy others' property rights. Closer inspection of contracts too shows that the notion that they advance the mutual interests of both parties to the agreement is often illusory. Powerful actors employ standardized contracts and offer their customers a take-it-or-leave-it option. As a result, contracts tend to reflect the interests of one party more than the other. Especially in the digital age, contracts legally empower not data producers but Big Tech, not least because information technology makes contracting at scale much easier while fragmenting and marginalizing the bargaining power of customers as well as labor. The law largely ignores these developments and instead continues to assume the freedom to contract and formal equality of the parties. This unrealistic assumption justifies allowing formal consent to suffice for subjecting millions of consumers and workers to the dictates of powerful corporations.

4

Access to Legal Coercion

Every society faces the challenge of controlling violence.[1] Social life falls apart and economic prosperity dwindles if society does not limit the use of violence and establish when, how, and by whom it can legitimately be used.[2] The modern nation-state is credited with having centralized the means of coercion in the hands of the state. To secure internal peace, the state banned self-help and feuds.[3] And to secure external peace, it built standing armies and found ways to fund them.[4] The power to execute coercive violence was taken out of the hands of individuals and clans and placed in the hands of designated institutions of the state, foremost among them the police, courts, and bailiffs, but later also regulators.[5]

States have not succeeded in completely consolidating control over the means of coercion. Power vacuums in the aftermath of wars and collapsing empires created ideal conditions for the rise of the Mafia and other organized criminal organizations.[6] The phenomenon of "failed states" reflects the loss of centralized control over the means of coercion together with the inability to forge consensus on how a country should be run.[7] As Charles Tilly has noted, state-making bears an eerie resemblance to organized crime. Struggling to secure their dominance, warriors had to make concessions to challengers and their allies.[8] In his account, these concessions laid the foundations for checks on power—from the Magna Carta (1215) all the way to modern constitutions.[9]

Centralizing coercion creates its own problems, however. Having gained the capacity to preserve peace internally as well as externally, the state may turn around and use its newly gained powers against any challenger to suppress all actions as it pleases.[10] This Hobbesian dilemma has been addressed at least in part by checks and balances and accountability mechanisms built into constitutions.[11] These measures have been remarkably successful in containing state power. An important reason might be that not all control rights over the means of coercion were vested with a central agent. Private actors had access to them as long as they used the channels that the law—in particular, procedural law—provided. These rules condition access by requiring that claimants have a legally recognizable interest, that they be eligible to fight for their own rights, and that the courts have jurisdiction over the matter. These conditions are usually justified as measures to ensure that frivolous lawsuits are kept at bay. As we will see, however, they also set the stage for winners and losers in individual disputes, but even more importantly, in the struggle over the rules that determine who is right and who has to yield. Law enforcement does not reach all spheres of social life. This may be viewed as a sign of respect for individual autonomy, but it often creates room for private government that lacks the kinds of constraints that modern constitutionalism has imposed on state power. Wielders of private power may not command prisons or armies, but their actions can nonetheless be coercive because they are not constrained by law or because they have mastered the art of accessing the coercive powers of the state to constrain others.

Some areas of social life, the family and to some extent the firm, were in the past off-limits and protected as private zones with only limited legal oversight. Under the common law, the head of the family had the power to "chastise" or "correct" the behavior of his wife, his children, and the animals that belonged to his household, including by physical means.[12] And although legal doctrine limited his powers to "moderate corrections," in practice, courts rarely intervened, citing familial privacy.[13] If conducted within marriage, even violent offenses such as rape were until fairly recently exempted from criminal prosecution in many jurisdictions—and in some jurisdictions, they still are.[14] Slave owners too were largely immune from prosecution for the violence they inflicted on their slaves. As owners of human bodies, they used and also abused those bodies. And although the killing or rape of slaves was not officially sanctioned, there was little redress as a matter of practice.[15] In short, property rights in their slaves created spheres of autonomy for the slave owners, but spheres of violence for the slaves themselves.

Times have changed. Slavery has been outlawed in most countries, and most states afford women and children legal protection against an abusive spouse or father. Still, much autonomy is still given to subgroups in society, including religious communities, to govern their own affairs, even when their conduct is in tension with the fundamental normative principles of the political community, including gender equality.[16] State law has had a hard time penetrating patriarchal structures, and many statutes that were enacted to change them have remained dead-letter law.[17] Companies are also sites of private government where investors and management rule over labor as their agents.[18] Labor law limits what employers can legally do, but law on the books does not guarantee implementation; laws can be difficult to police, especially when the beneficiaries of legal protection are economically dependent on those who ignore it. Loopholes in the law—intentional or not—further expand the power of enterprises over their workers. In the United States, firms are obliged under the regime of the National Labor Relations Board to negotiate with workers only with respect to "wages, hours, and terms and conditions of employment"; managerial prerogatives, including whether to shut down an enterprise to avoid unionization, are disclaimed from this mandate.[19] Other jurisdictions grant labor greater participatory rights, including participation in workers' councils and company boards. Their voice may not be as strong as that of investors, but codetermination in Germany, for example, gives them access to information and with it the ability to mobilize against strategic change.[20] How far the law reaches, whom it protects, and how effective these mechanisms are is thus not preordained. It is a matter of political choice and of normative commitments to ensure that freedom is not reserved for those with more economic power.

Occasionally the law refuses to enforce a claim because it deems the claim to be immoral or to violate some fundamental principles of justice. Many legal systems refuse to enforce contracts for paid sex because they deem prostitution immoral, for example. Other contracts have been more readily cleansed of social stigma. Wagers, or speculative transactions in which parties bet on a financial outcome without holding the underlying asset (equivalent to taking out fire insurance on your neighbor's house), were deemed unenforceable under the common law. This did not prevent or eliminate speculation in markets, but it kept a lid on speculation because parties faced a real risk of getting stiffed by their counterparties. Once this stigma was removed in the United States by the Commodity Futures Modernization Act in 2000, use of derivatives (the most fashionable wagers of the day) skyrocketed.[21] As this illustrates, legal enforceability—the option to take another party to court for breach of contract—is the backbone for high-stakes markets, notwithstanding attempts to characterize them as self-governing.

Ubi ius ibi remedium—where there is a right, there is a remedy—is an old saying that really means that where there is a *legal* right, there must be a *legal* remedy.[22] Not just any right counts—only rights that are recognized by law. A property right, a claim for breach of contract, or a right to compensation for damages (a tort claim), can serve as an entry ticket to litigation, but only if the claim meets the conditions that statutory and case law establish for the right in question. People may think that they have a property right to their own data, or to the money in their bank accounts, or that as victims of pollution they may sue the company that caused it, but the law often thinks differently.

Plaintiffs who have sued tech companies for collecting their data without consent, for example, have seen many of their claims rejected because the law does not recognize a property right in data—at least not in the hands of the data creators.[23] Claims based on a violation of the right to privacy have also been regularly denied because much of the information collected is deemed to be outside one's sphere of privacy. This includes one's address or location. Collecting such information, courts have argued, is "routine commercial behavior" that does not breach any social norms.[24] But this behavior has become routine only because the law failed to protect individuals from this kind of intrusion early enough to forestall its normalization.

More generally, "standing" rules that courts have developed to determine who has a legitimate claim to bring an action have created a complex set of hurdles that plaintiffs must overcome if they want to have their day in court. Standing rules are not mentioned in the constitutional provisions that guarantee access to the law or in civil-procedure law. Article III of the U.S. Constitution puts it plainly and simply: "The judicial power shall extend to all cases, in law and equity, arising under this Constitution, the laws of the United States, and treaties."[25] Yet courts have insisted that a case "in law" is only a case that qualifies under existing statutory and case law, and that this means that a plaintiff must show "injury in fact," which must be "concrete" as well as "particularized." What these words mean specifically and how to distinguish between them is not apparent, not even, it seems, to the justices on the Supreme Court. According to Justice Samuel Alito in *Spokeo v. Robins,* an injury is particularized if it is "actual or imminent, not conjectural or hypothetical," and it is concrete when it is "*de facto,*" that is, "it must actually exist."[26] The difference between "not conjectural or hypothetical" and "really existing" still remains elusive, but this did not help the plaintiff whose case was dismissed.

What makes this case interesting is not only its interpretative acrobatics but the legal right in question. In a class-action suit, the lead plaintiff complained about a search engine that misrepresented his personal affairs, including his image, age, marital status, and training. He invoked the Fair Credit Reporting Act of 1970, which Congress passed to protect individuals from errors in such information, especially as it affects their credit rating.[27] This act also gives affected individuals a right to sue whoever disseminates misinformation about them and does not impose the kinds of conditions that the majority opinion written by Justice Alito required. In their dissent, Justices Ruth Bader Ginsburg and Sonia Sotomayor insisted that Congress has the power to create such rights and that courts should not impose their own criteria, especially when they have not done so consistently.[28]

Courts are not only the primary interpreters of the law but also the guardians of the courthouse, which keeps the key to the means of coercion. It is easy to see why some restrictions are necessary to avoid courts being flooded with frivolous lawsuits. It is equally important to ensure that the entry requirements do not bar rightful claims, as this leaves plaintiffs without legal recourse. This outcome is particularly worrisome when entry criteria are sufficiently obscure to give judges a lot of leeway to throw out cases. The importance of access rules to legal process was even more apparent under Roman law: Only those actions that the magistrate had specified would give the claimant a court hearing. As Ernest Metzger, an expert in Roman law put it, "To have an action meant that a person was entitled to legal process."[29] The list of actions a magistrate would endorse changed over time, and it was not uncommon for some would-be plaintiffs to lobby a magistrate to accept a novel claim under an existing "action" or for a new action to be added to the list.[30] In a legal system that did not clearly distinguish between rights and legal process, accessing the legal process was key. Still, in rights-centered capitalist regimes, a right on its own does not make one's case either.

Without standing and without meeting other procedural entry requirements, there is simply no legal remedy.

A final barrier to the courthouse, and thus to the means of coercion, is that only eligible rights bearers can launch a legal claim. Children and incapacitated persons, for example, are not eligible to bring a claim without the help of their parents or guardians. In many jurisdictions, women became eligible to own property only in the mid-nineteenth century (even though they had long been eligible to sell their labor), and debt finance took even longer to become gender neutral. In 1848, New York became the first U.S. state to allow married women to own property.[31] Race, too, has long affected whether an individual has a right and is able to enforce it. Enslaved Black people were not considered persons with the same rights as whites. Some slaves who, against the odds, had attained literacy fought for their rights in court, and at times with success, but most were without effective legal protection.[32] The call for former slaves (and their descendants) to be compensated for the exploitation they suffered under slavery remains hotly contested in the United States to this day.[33] Emancipation, it seems, was considered enough of a remedy. Not slaves, but slave *owners,* received compensation, certainly in the United Kingdom but also in parts of the United States, because abolition, the argument went, was expropriation.[34] Even where no compensation was paid, slave owners made up remarkably quickly for their loss in economic value. By contrast, the formerly enslaved never did, and for reasons that can at least in part be attributed to the law: to its failure to afford them adequate legal protection and its willingness to shield others who violated them.

Emancipation did not, and on its own could not, give Black Americans real freedom. They did not have access to resources to become successful. To be eligible to obtain public land for free under the Homestead Act of 1862, they had to move West. Lacking the resources, many had no option but to stay where they had been and earn a living as sharecroppers.[35] Three years after emancipation, the Fourteenth Amendment was adopted to prohibit states from depriving *any person* of "life, liberty, or property" without "due process of Law" and tasked federal courts with enforcing these rights.[36] There were good reasons not to trust state courts on these matters given that in many Southern states, legislatures and courts continued to mobilize state law to entrench racism. This was the era of Jim Crow, of denying Black people access to the courts and fair hearings, and of the police and the courts openly condoning physical violence against Black people by withholding the state's means of coercion to prevent lynching or punish its perpetrators. Whiteness was a kind of property right, as Cheryl Harris put it, another case of "status property."[37]

These examples show how most humans had to struggle for centuries in order to be recognized as legitimate bearers of rights, the same rights that white males often took for granted as their "natural rights." The modern business corporation too was adorned with the right to own property, to contract, and to sue and be sued in its own name from inception. This was what it meant to be a "legal person." Even unincorporated business organizations, such as partnerships, can today claim rights in the name of the company rather than its owners in many legal systems.[38] No doubt, this makes it easier for such businesses to protect their rights, but similar privileges are not necessarily extended to others, such as collective labor organizations or victims of environmental degradation.[39] Recent movements to endow nature with similar rights have often been met with ridicule; inanimate things allegedly cannot be rights bearers.[40] Yet this has never prevented corporations from claiming these rights, indeed from expanding them to the canon of human rights, including the right to free speech and religious rights.

Because of the central importance of civil procedure for rights equality, class-action suits were created in the United States in

1938 in the new Federal Rules of Civil Procedure and expanded in 1966.[41] In a class action, a single individual who is deemed representative of a class can sue on the class's behalf, with the effect that every class member will get a share but will also be legally bound by the outcome of the case.[42] This altered the legal playing field between small, often dispersed, plaintiffs and large corporations and makes it easier for consumers, employees, lessees, and others to litigate collectively.

When the rule allowing class actions was first enacted, many believed that these rights would rarely be used. Instead, they became an important tool for consolidating claims and asserting the rights of consumers and shareholders vis-à-vis corporations. The "golden age" of the class-action suit was the first decade after the rules supporting these actions were expanded in 1966. Cases proliferated, to the dismay of the corporate world, and the remedies that had to be paid out skyrocketed. Empirical evidence cautions against drawing the conclusion that the weak and the poor—rather than the plaintiffs' bar (i.e., lawyers representing such claims), for example—were the primary beneficiaries of this legal tool.[43] As Linda Mullenix put it, attorneys often posture as the "white knights (or white-hatted cowboys) who are protectors of the down-trodden victims of corporate misfeasance and greed," but she also hinted at their darker side as bounty hunters.[44] In the United States, these attorneys work on contingency fees and get a share of the amount they secure for their clients, which provides an incentive for them to find cases, locate eligible plaintiffs, and bring suit. In theory, these incentives should benefit parties who lack the resources to litigate, but they have a perhaps unintended consequence: attorneys oppose the use of regulation to address worker safety, preferring the litigation path, which is more lucrative to them.[45] Still, even if attorneys benefit more than the average class members, class actions have contributed to better policing of corporate actions that negatively affect parties whose claims are too small to make individual litigation worthwhile and who face collective-action problems that this procedural tool can help overcome.[46]

The best evidence for the impact of class actions on the corporate world is the stern opposition to them expressed by the U.S. Chamber of Commerce. In the 1980s, it launched a counteroffensive that found sympathetic justices on the Supreme Court. They helped roll back key pillars that had made class-action suits such powerful policing devices. First on the block was discovery, which was a central piece of the 1938 reforms of the Federal Rules of Civil Procedure and gave litigants the right to access critical information in the possession of the defendant.[47] Next, the Court heightened the pleading standards for class-action suits—not only in securities class actions, where strike suits had become common, but also for consumer and employee actions, where they were less so.[48] The Court was not alone in rolling back the civil-procedure reforms of the 1930s. Congress went along as well, adopting legislation that tightened the standing rules for fraud actions after appellate courts diverged on what plaintiffs in a class-action suit had to show to demonstrate intentional wrongdoing by the defendant.[49] Yet Congress was also divided over the issue, and the legislation that it passed was so ambiguous that it resulted in yet another circuit split—that is, contradictory interpretations of the same statute by different circuit courts.[50] The issue remains far from settled, but the example demonstrates how procedural rules that determine access to the courts can shape the power balance between different economic actors and shows the critical role that courts play in tilting the balance one way or the other.

Globalized markets appear to defy the importance of law and the state's coercive powers for capitalist economies. These markets seem to exist outside territorial states and their legal and regulatory apparatuses, as the free space in which private parties meet and negotiate the terms of their agreement without state tutelage or constraints. In fact, global markets are deeply structured in law, significantly and in large measure by the parties that choose the law that governs their transactions.[51] The ability to pick and choose the law by which one wishes to be governed, and along with it the courts that will settle disputes, is a feature of capitalist legal regimes, which transferred enormous power to the hands of private actors. States adopted conflict-of-law rules and endorsed choice-of-forum clauses in the belief that this would grease the wheels of international commerce, but in effect, they franchised for free their law and enforcement powers to private parties.

A franchise is a contract in which one company makes available its name, recipes, or production manuals to an independent contractor who runs and controls the business for a fee or a share of the profits of the franchisor—and critically, under the franchisor's name.[52] Robert Hockett and Saule Omarova used the concept to describe the money-creation process in capitalist systems, which has largely been outsourced to private banks.[53] In a similar vein, I use the term to denote the practice of states offering their coercive powers to enforce the rulings of private tribunals and foreign courts. States exercise far less control over their franchisees than a typical franchisor does. They do not select the law or the tribunals whose rulings they will enforce, but leave the choice to private parties. They don't even subject franchisees such as arbitral tribunals to quality control under their own legal standards. International law requires them to enforce the rulings of foreign and international arbitral tribunals as long as those tribunals observe some basic procedural principles. Only in exceptional cases, when a ruling violates fundamental principles of their legal order (*ordre publique*), are state courts allowed to deny the enforcement of a ruling.[54] Recently, the franchise has been extended from arbitral tribunals to foreign courts, which has made court rulings portable and fostered transnational forum shopping.[55]

Historically, the right to a judge was fought for long and hard, and not just in criminal but also in civil matters. The notion in modern law that individuals have rights was interpreted to include the right to an independent and impartial court. As countries democratized, they expanded access to the courts and revised their procedural rules to ensure fair, cheap, and transparent proceedings.[56] Oftentimes this included additional protection and legal ammunition for the weaker party, such as legal aid, the use of discovery, or collective-action suits. The very success of reforms that were aimed at democratizing justice has helped undermine their effectiveness over time, mostly because the allocation of resources to the judiciary did not keep up with the growing demand for legal justice. The number of lawsuits and the related costs for staffing the court system skyrocketed, which resulted in overworked courts and massive backlogs.[57] Instead of investing in the judiciary, many countries curtailed access to it. They streamlined their civil-procedure rules, limited the number of oral hearings, and increased the threshold value needed to bring cases or appeal them to a higher court. And although justice delayed is also justice denied, these reforms effectively limited access to coercive law enforcement for many smaller claims.[58]

In some cases, the rollback has gone even further by effectively privatizing dispute settlement. The U.S. Supreme Court sanctioned mandatory arbitration clauses not just in commercial transactions between fairly sophisticated entrepreneurs who tend to have competent legal advice, but also in standardized consumer and labor contracts.[59] In a leading case that set the tone for what was to come, Justice Antonin Scalia interpreted the Federal Arbitration Act of 1925 as revealing Congress's intent to prioritize arbitration over litigation—without offering any evidence to support this claim.[60] In fact, before the adoption of the act in 1925, U.S. courts had regularly denied the enforceability of mandatory arbitration provisions.[61] In Scalia's new and unsubstantiated interpretation of history, the Federal Arbitration Act was intended to preempt federal and state legislation prohibiting parties with superior bargaining power from imposing mandatory arbitration clauses on consumers who lack bargaining power and often do not fully understand the implications of accepting these contracts.[62] In subsequent cases, the Court upheld mandatory arbitration provisions in employment contracts that preclude class actions.[63]

These developments have effectively denied entire classes of cases, indeed entire social classes, access to the courts. A recent study of consumer finance contracts by the Consumer Financial Protection Bureau (CFPB) revealed that the majority of consumer financial services contracts had mandatory arbitration clauses: 53 percent of credit cards, 44.4 percent of checking accounts, over 82 percent of prepaid cards, 98.5 percent of storefront payday loans, and 99.9 percent of mobile wireless contracts.[64] According to the same CFPB study, between 87 and 100 percent of consumer financial contracts included clauses that "expressly did not allow arbitration to proceed on a class basis."[65] The data likely understates the actual incidence of mandatory arbitration clauses. The study's scope is limited to consumer contracts in finance; moreover, private contracts are not easily accessible, which makes it difficult to collect data.

The European Union has pursued a different path and therefore makes for an interesting comparison. It too has turned to arbitration to ease the burden on courts, but not without developing a comprehensive regulatory framework for alternative dispute resolution (ADR) in consumer disputes.[66] Its stated goal was to make ADR accessible for consumers as an option but without denying them access to the courts. Individual member states may make arbitration mandatory for businesses if consumers so desire, but so far, relatively few states have done so. As a result, ADR has not really taken off in Europe. Apparently, businesses are far less eager to move to arbitration when the choice is in the consumers' hands and when arbitral tribunals are well supervised.[67] The comparison between the United States and the European Union suggests that the issue is not so much whether arbitration or litigation is more efficient or equitable for solving disputes in consumer contracts, but whether the business side can control its terms. It also confirms the central importance of procedural rules for the balance of power between different actors and the ease with which they can access the centralized means of coercion. When states establish these rules, they face a choice: They can tilt the balance in favor of powerful corporate actors under the guise of legal neutrality and allow such actors to use mandatory arbitration clauses to preclude their counterparties from accessing the courts. Or they can do the opposite and use procedural rules to strengthen the hand of structurally weaker parties, as the Federal Rules of Civil Procedure of 1938 did in the United States and EU rules on consumer arbitration have done more recently. These choices over matters of procedural law deeply affect material outcomes. In the memorable words of Congressman John Dingell on the relative importance of procedural versus substantive rules: "I let you write the substance, you let me write the procedure, and I'll screw you every time."[68]

A legal system that is backed by the consolidated means of coercion socializes the costs of protecting rights. With such a system in place, private actors do not have to hire their own security guards to protect their resources. Instead, they can rely on the law and its enforceability, which, like other public goods, they get essentially free. All they need to do is pay the actual costs of litigation in a specific dispute should they be involved in one or the fees that regulators might charge them. As long as most others follow the rules most of the time, they can effectively free ride on the legal system. Not all legal commitments must be enforced coercively; most are complied with voluntarily. Still, the enforcement option makes formal law a powerful tool for scaling economic relations beyond the boundaries of communities within which social norms and mutual monitoring mechanisms suffice for maintaining social order.[69] The shadow of formal law does more than just expand the scope of socioeconomic relations; it also deepens existing power relations and offers additional tools to entrench them. This can be shown by examining self-help and self-enforcing mechanisms that are said to have existed in "the state of nature"—an idealized world without a legal system and a state to back it. These mechanisms have not disappeared with the expansion of formal law and are still widely used today, only with the added power of state enforcement.[70]

A good example of enforcing commitments, such as the commitment to repay a loan, without having to rely on a legal enforcement apparatus is hostage taking. A "hostage" is something of value to the debtor that she delivers to the creditor, who can destroy it should she renege on the loan.[71] A hostage works as a psychological bond, not, at least not primarily, as a substitute asset that could be sold if the debtor defaulted on her loan, because the value of the hostage is often personal and does not translate into pecuniary value. This may sound like something from a bygone age, but formal legal pledges, like mortgages or guarantees, can also have substantial personal value to the debtor over and above their pecuniary value. A house is not only an asset but also a home. This is why banks so readily lend to prospective homeowners; they know that few will risk default on their mortgage.[72] And yet, the same banks also rely on law and the state's coercive powers to evict an owner in default should she fall behind in her payments. Hostage taking may work without state power, but both work all the better in combination.

The old mechanism of "hands-tying" has also benefited from the addition of legal backing.[73] Its purpose is to make it nearly impossible for either party to escape the binding nature of a contract. Granting a creditor automatic access to the debtor's future cash flows can be described as a hands-tying mechanism because it makes it impossible for the debtor to default and irresistible for the creditor to keep lending. Walmart introduced such a mechanism in the United States, offering its employees the ability to use earned-but-unpaid wages as collateral for a loan, and allowing creditors to access those wages once paid to satisfy their claims.[74] For employees, attempting to escape the mounting debt burden by terminating employment may be more costly than seeing their meager paychecks—often too small to meet daily expenses—dwindle before their eyes. Conversely, creditors may have little choice but to keep the tab open and provide debtors with enough liquidity to make it to the next paycheck in order to secure their own repayment. Both parties have tied their hands. This and the hostage example also suggest that the "state of nature" is still upon us. Formal legal systems did not replace but incorporated these commitment devices into formal law, adding the state's coercive powers for upholding them. The law put its stamp of approval on mechanisms that were born out of might, and made them a right.

Recent developments in the use of digitized binding agreements, or smart contracts, threaten to make matters even more lopsided in favor of sellers or creditors over buyers and debtors.[75] Once put into motion, smart contracts run their course like a train that has left the station and can be stopped only by emergency measures. In the words of Kevin Werbach and Nicolas Cornell, "Smart contracts attempt to atomize the contractual process. They formally strip away the time dimension of interactions between the parties, and the uncertainties of future judicial resolution."[76] In this way, they tilt the balance further in favor of the party with the power to impose its contractual terms on all others. Payment is secured before delivery, and the burden of challenging the quality of goods and services falls squarely on the recipient, who no longer has the option to withhold or reduce payment in case the other side underperforms. Smart contracts can therefore be said to complete the process of disembedding legal from social relations, unmitigated by morals or normative principles.[77] Form—in this case, the legal combined with the digital form—triumphs over substance and over morals.[78]

This chapter has shown that access to the means of coercion, which have been consolidated and placed in the hands of the state and its enforcement apparatus, is available not just to state but also to private actors. However, this access is highly uneven and maps onto entrenched relations of economic and social power. Private actors with sufficient resources can choose when and how often to litigate. They are in this game for the long term and for shaping its rules. By contrast, less resourceful parties struggle to have their cases heard by a court and rarely have enough money or stamina to appeal a case, much less relitigate the same issue over and over again. Attempts to level the playing field by introducing discovery rules and class-action suits or requiring arbitration to be rule bound and customer friendly have had some success, at least in the medium term. However, they did not succeed in ensuring equal access to the consolidated means of coercion in real, not just formal, terms.

5

Legal Arbitrage

In finance, arbitrage refers to the idea of exploiting opportunities for profit while guarding against losses, or to "[t]he simultaneous purchase and sale of the same, or essentially similar, security in two different markets for advantageously different prices."[1] When applied to law, the same idea can be expressed as the simultaneous securing of law's protection and power for one's own interests while avoiding its costs and constraints.[2] Legal arbitrage overlaps with the more frequently used concept of regulatory arbitrage, also defined as "formal compliance with rules while violating their spirit," or taking advantage of legal inconsistencies.[3] I prefer the broader concept of legal arbitrage because it clarifies that the practice is much more widespread and affects many more areas of law than just regulation.

In a frictionless world without information costs and with full knowledge of the future, there would be little room for legal arbitrage. With full knowledge of all possible future contingencies, lawmakers would simply write complete law. In a complex world with information costs, law is inherently incomplete—more so than contracts.[4] And without full knowledge of the future, even the best-designed legislation will need to be adapted to changing circumstances. Additional frictions can result from political compromise and drafting errors. Some laws are born with "multiple personality disorder"—unresolved political controversies are baked into them, which creates ample space for interpretation as well as repurposing.[5] This too is unavoidable in competitive political systems, although its severity increases with political divisiveness. Overlapping legal systems are also an important source of legal arbitrage. In federal systems with state and federal law, for example, even the most careful delineation of jurisdiction will not eliminate the possibility that the same issues might be regulated by both state and federal authorities. Similarly, in the world of transnational commerce and investment, different states offer different menus of laws or impose their mandatory rules on actors that are also subject to the laws of a different jurisdiction. In all these cases, frictions between rules are almost inevitable, and these frictions can be exploited for legal arbitrage.

Economic theory recognizes that contracts are incomplete. Under conditions of fundamental uncertainty, it is impossible for the contracting parties to anticipate all future contingencies and provide for them in their contracts.[6] Trying to do so would be cost prohibitive and ultimately futile. It follows that law must also be incomplete, arguably even more so. Law is meant to cover not just a single transaction or long-term contract between two parties, but many different cases; it applies to a multiplicity of actors, transactions, and circumstances, not only today but far into the future.[7] Statutes rarely have sunset provisions; most continue to linger on the books even when no longer relevant and can be excavated to solve future cases, including cases for which they may not have been intended. A law is a law, and unless it is repealed it remains "good" law.

Still, lawmakers have some discretion over how incomplete law shall be. They can make it open-ended or highly specific.[8] For example, general principles or standards—such as "reasonableness," "fairness," or "materiality"—leave more room for interpretation than specific rules that state more precisely the threshold of actions that may or may not be allowed. By contrast, more precise rules may fail to capture behavior that deviates only slightly from the wording of the rule. In general, standards tend to be overinclusive, whereas rules are underinclusive. Of course, not all actions that might violate a law will be challenged by a state agent or private actor. Resource constraints stand in the way, as do entry barriers to litigation, as discussed in the previous chapter.

It follows that the choice between standards and rules affects different actors differently. As a rule of thumb, the business community tends to prefer rules over standards, as reflected in its constant call for "legal certainty." When the law is precise, it becomes more calculable—a big plus in light of the many other uncertainties that economic actors face. Being underinclusive, precise rules also create a lot of space for law avoidance. In contrast, broadly stated standards place a lot of power in the hands of law enforcers who will judge after the fact whether a particular action has violated the standard. However, they can act only if and when a case comes to their attention, which makes their influence and power ultimately dependent on litigators. Identifying the true beneficiaries of law's incompleteness therefore depends on the propensity of different actors to challenge the legality of an action, and to do so not only once but repeatedly. Resources matter for litigation, as we have seen in the previous chapters; actors who are secure in their existing legal empowerments will need fewer resources than actors who are trying to advance new frontiers of legal interpretation to further their interests. Investing these resources can have big payoffs, but only for those who have the resources to bet on a rule change in their favor. For them, the costs of excavating old laws and repurposing those laws to satisfy their needs can be a worthy undertaking, whereas actors with more limited resources will shy away from it.

A good example is the use of the partnership form for organizing businesses to engage in tax arbitrage. It is one of the most commonly used legal forms because it requires no charter and no registration. The law simply presumes a partnership once two or more people get together for a profit-seeking activity. Because partnerships are the default legal form for most small businesses, Congress decided in the 1950s to afford them certain tax privileges. The immediate impact of this law was moderate. However, the partnership form has become much more popular in recent years—not, however, for small businesses, but for investors wishing to shield profits from taxation by channeling their share through the partnership form and taking advantage of the tax benefits originally intended for small self-employed entrepreneurs. The attraction of using the partnership form lies in the fact that profits and losses can be allocated to different partners as the partners wish. Shifting makes the most sense for partners with high tax burdens, but these are not your typical small entrepreneur. Only 3 percent of high-value partnership groups engage in tax shifting of this kind, but they are responsible for most of it. In dollar terms, "the top 1% of shifters account for 99% of the total dollars shifted."[9] To state the obvious, it takes a lawyer to pull this off, and that adds to the cost of taking advantage of these structures, which favors the rich. The example also suggests that combining and recombining different legal institutions (tax law with organizational law, for example) offers good legal-arbitrage opportunities.

An examination of the practice of legal arbitrage cautions against the idea that the best-intentioned law reforms will result in lasting change that was actually intended. History sometimes has "switching points" that create an opening for reform.[10] However, even if these reforms materialize, legal-arbitrage techniques may thwart their effect. The tax subsidy for partnerships mentioned above reflects a social consensus in the 1950s that smaller firms deserved state support. In the end, the reforms produced the greatest windfall for powerful economic actors with lawyers at their side who repurposed these reforms, and did so decades after the law was enacted. Humans, being strategic actors, do not just passively respond to a given set of constraints (as many economic models assume); they strive to shape institutions to their liking. Legal arbitrage can work in many ways: As in the example just given, it can be used to take advantage of tax benefits that originally targeted different constituencies; it can also be used to avoid the costs of regulation or to opt into a legal regime that offers benefits that others don't. Importantly, legal arbitrage works without explicit legal change. No legislature needs to enact a new law, and no court has to overrule a precedent. Much of legal arbitrage operates by taking advantage of frictions within existing law and asserting that the advanced strategy is legal. In this way, it contributes to the process of incremental institutional change, which may be small and even slow, but in its cumulative effects can have far-reaching consequences.

Kathleen Thelen and Wolfgang Streeck have critiqued the theory of institutional change that dominates in the new institutional economics. The theory holds that change tends to be path dependent, which means that the system is unlikely to veer from a course that was set by earlier choices, and which leaves exogenous shocks as the only realistic opportunity for radical or transformative change. Thelen and Streeck argue instead that institutional change is an ongoing process that may be incremental but can result in transformative change. They also classify different modes of incremental institutional change, which they label displacement, layering, drift, conversion, and exhaustion.[11] Conversion is the clearest example of strategic action aimed at repurposing an existing legal institution for a new purpose that fits one's own needs—just as a tax subsidy for small businesses helped sophisticated investors shift their taxes decades later. Drift, which captures the idea that society evolves without updating its institutions, could be the result of collective amnesia or a conscious choice not to update a law in order to undermine its efficacy. The federal minimum wage in the United States, which has remained at $7.25 since 2009 without updates for the cost of living and inflation, is an illustration of how a law that is not adapted to changing circumstances simply fades out of relevance.[12]

The ability of actors to take advantage of legal-arbitrage opportunities cannot be legislated away, because the inherent incompleteness of law and the dynamics of continuous social and technological change invariably create frictions within existing law that lend themselves to this practice. The coding of capital takes advantage of these frictions—indeed, they enable the coding of ever new assets as capital: The legal rules that applied to chattel property were extended in the sixteenth and seventeenth centuries to real property in order to transform land from a common resource into a commodity; the corporate form was repurposed from a device to broaden the investor base for capital-intensive industries into an ATM for shareholders; and intellectual-property rights were used to generate data and monopolize control over that data even though data itself cannot be patented.[13] Repurposing the law in this way works when the law is interpreted in a highly positivistic fashion that seeks compliance only with the letter of the law and strips out its purpose and normative foundation. The only defense against an extensive, if not abusive, use of legal arbitrage is therefore the assertion that purpose matters, as does a solid normative foundation that respects individual autonomy but also the rights and needs of others.

The incompleteness of law is only one reason for legal arbitrage; another is the plurality of normative orders, both domestically and internationally. Multiple, overlapping legal regimes operate in every state: constitutional and ordinary, public and private, statutory and case, and central and municipal, but also formal and informal, state and religious, and in federations, federal and state. Frictions between these legal orders create additional legal-arbitrage opportunities.[14] These arbitrage opportunities can be reduced by rules that create hierarchies among the various legal regimes, such as "constitutional law trumps statutory law," "federal law preempts state law," or "local law shall prevail over national or supranational law," as required by the subsidiary principle in European law.[15] Eliminating all frictions, however, is impossible, especially in the transnational realm. To minimize frictions, the principle of comity in international law requires states to limit the reach of domestic law to their own territory. However, when violations of domestic law take place extraterritorially, such as anticompetitive conduct that is organized abroad or securities fraud that is committed against foreign investors, countries frequently extend the reach of their laws and in this way add additional frictions.[16]

Private law also varies enough among countries to create room for legal arbitrage when transactions are conducted across jurisdictional borders. To minimize disruptions, countries often harmonize or standardize the law formally through treaty law, or sometimes by soft law such as codes of conduct or model laws, which operate through persuasion, not coercion. In the United States, soft standardization of private law, jurisdiction over which lies in the hands of the individual states, has been the preferred strategy.[17] By contrast, the European Union pursued a more ambitious harmonization program for decades before realizing that this was too cumbersome and time consuming.[18] It has therefore shifted emphasis to harmonizing choice-of-law rules (or international private law) in core areas, such as contracts and torts.[19] These rules ignore differences in the substance of domestic legal orders. Instead, they streamline the rules that select the legal order that shall govern a case if more than one is in play, and in this way they try to ensure that the applicable law will be the same even if courts in different member states are called upon to determine it.

Harmonizing all law in the European Union or globally has been and will remain impossible and would be undesirable. There is nothing wrong with a plurality of norms and different preferences that are expressed in laws and regulations. Streamlining all law to reduce transaction costs for global capital is not a value that should suppress the preferences of different communities and polities. In fact, even if all formal law were standardized, differences in the underlying norms, values, and practices, as well as different patterns of social change, affect the meaning and application of the law, and this would invariably result in different uses and meanings of these rules. Creating a single unified legal order would also eliminate legal experimentation as an important source for legal innovation.

If legal orders are inherently plural internally and in relation to one another, legal arbitrage cannot be avoided. This suggests that legal arbitrage is not a distinct feature of capitalist law. The critical issue is that within capitalist law, not everyone can benefit equally from legal-arbitrage opportunities; some are subject to legal standards that are imposed on them—not necessarily by states but by economic actors that seek to reduce their transaction costs and control those with whom they contract. For the more resourceful with good legal advice, large swaths of the law have become portable. They can shop for the rules and tribunals that are most amenable to them. Others are stuck with local law and boilerplate contracts and may not even know that they have a choice.

At the global level, legal arbitrage is the order of the day, because savvy actors can take advantage of *"un vaste bricolage normatif,"* a "vast normative do-it-yourself" (DIY) in Jean-Bernard Auby's translation.[20] DIY shows where agency is located in the global legal order. Agency lies not with public lawmakers, such as state legislatures or courts, but with norm entrepreneurs who mix and match the vast normative material from the different jurisdictions available to them: hard and soft law, international law, and the many domestic laws that are the product of every nation-state, plus subnational law. Normative bricolage is not only a feature of the global order. Legal pluralism is inherent to all complex legal orders that leave lawmaking or law enforcement to a plurality of agents.[21] It is also normatively desirable because it allows communities to express their own normative preferences in policy choices and legal rules. For actors seeking every loophole and every opportunity to combine and recombine legal devices to advance their own interests, however, this inherent feature of complex legal systems offers great arbitrage opportunities. They can claim formal legality with at least one order and wait for others to catch up with them and challenge their strategy.

Conflict of laws (also referred to as international private law), is the body of law that was meant to bring some order into this bricolage. It is part of every domestic legal order and specifies criteria for determining which jurisdiction's laws apply to a given case if more than one jurisdiction's laws might be in play. The reasons for this can be manifold. The parties to a dispute might hail from different countries, and even if they don't, they might have encountered each other elsewhere; or they might have selected a legal system other than their own because it promised neutrality or offered features that their own legal system was lacking.

There was already a need for conflict-of-law rules before the rise of the nation-state. Long-distance trade crossed the boundaries of cities, regions, fiefdoms, and kingdoms, each with its own set of legal rules.[22] To avoid having to deal with many different and unfamiliar legal orders, these traders relied on kinship ties or trusted middlemen to sort out disputes that might arise along the way.[23] This limited the scope of possible trading relations to these networks.[24] Alternatively, they sold their goods at central trade fairs. Cities that organized these fairs often imposed their own local law on foreign merchants. Upon request, they would also grant foreign merchants who originated from the same place the privilege to use their own law to settle disputes among themselves.[25]

The imposition of local law created a level playing field, at least among all *foreign* merchants who were all equally unfamiliar with the local law, and no individual could exploit his superior knowledge of another set of rules to the disadvantage of his trading partners. It may have given local merchants in the host city of the fair a comparative advantage and allowed local lawyers to seek a rent, but this was a minor price to pay in order to create a level playing field for the rest. Territorial states forged national legal systems from the bricolage of law that the particularist legal orders, which preceded them, left for them, and in this way reduced the plurality of legal systems within them. But they also created a new source of bricolage: their own national borders that demarcated their national legal systems, many of them containing mandatory rules for actors who transacted or held their property within their territory. These principles did not sit well with the globalization of commerce and investment; in fact, strictly adhering to the priority of national laws would have made globalization difficult.

Two paths were available to lead out of this dilemma: the harmonization of law across states or conflict-of-law rules with the implied expansion of private autonomy to pick and choose laws from among the many legal systems on offer. The European Union opted for the former, whereas the United States chose the latter in combination with recommendations for uniform standards in soft, not hard, law.[26] And for countries in the developing world, the World Bank and, to a lesser extent, the International Monetary Fund have pushed legal change advocating "best practice" laws, which invariably are the laws of more developed countries.[27] Harmonization is cumbersome and is complicated by the incompatibility of some legal institutions that might exist in one country but not in another, or different rules about what constitutes a valid right that are difficult to reconcile. Differences in legal culture, with political infighting, and national pride further added to the exceedingly slow process of harmonizing law within the European Union, which eventually gave priority to the standardization of conflict-of-law rules over attempts to harmonize substantive law.[28]

Legal harmonization necessarily entails a decrease in options to choose from. For advocates of economic efficiency and individual freedom, this smacks of paternalism.[29] But if everyone chose the law by which he or she wished to be governed, collective self-governance would be upended. It is therefore critical to ask who benefits and who loses from the choice of law in different constellations of power. Similarly, it is too easy to condemn legal standardization as suboptimal when compared with private choice, because it ignores whose interests are protected by standardization—for example, by offering a uniform sales or similar law that is available off-the-shelf for weaker or relatively uninformed parties.[30] Furthermore, the idea that private parties are best off when they can freely choose their own law ignores the impact that these choices have on society and on the law itself. Private autonomy in choice of law frequently produces hegemony of one legal system.

The U.S. legal system offers a glimpse at how the plurality of laws paired with choice of law produces legal hegemony. The core areas of private law, including property, contracts, and torts, lie within the jurisdiction of the individual states. This fosters plurality and lawmaking that is in line with local preferences. However, the commerce clause of the U.S. Constitution has been interpreted to prevent individual states from refusing to recognize the law of other states.[31] The combination of choice of law and a legal mandate to recognize and enforce foreign law (in this case the law of other states) has turned choice of law into a powerful opportunity for legal arbitrage, especially for resourceful actors. Moreover, it has created near legal monopolies as different states have sought to attract those parties that typically make these choices. Notably, Delaware remains the leader in corporate law because it has long played to the interests of corporate management, which controls the reincorporation decision.[32] Although Elon Musk convinced the shareholders of Tesla, the car company he leads, to reincorporate in Texas after he lost a legal dispute over his compensation in Delaware, this will hardly undermine the powerful network effects that decades of corporate-law jurisprudence in Delaware have produced.[33] In addition, the Delaware legislature stands ready to correct case law that threatens the state's dominance, as it did in enacting "pro-market" reforms in 2024 in an explicit rebuke of its judiciary.[34] Further, Delaware and South Carolina have attracted the banking and insurance sectors because they offer soft anti-usury rules that prohibit only excessively high interest rates, which can be imposed on the rest of the country.[35] Texas has positioned itself as the most attractive state for corporate bankruptcy, not for liquidating or even reorganizing firms, but for the "Texas two-step."[36] This is not a new country dance, but a legal maneuver that allows a corporation to avoid liability in mass tort actions by splitting itself into two companies and ring-fencing all its liabilities in one of them.

In Europe, the broadening of choice of law in corporate law has produced similar results. In 1999, the Court of Justice of the European Union began allowing corporations to select their place of incorporation irrespective of whether they do any business in that location.[37] This has resulted in the migration of new companies to the United Kingdom and the Netherlands in particular, to the detriment of countries with less flexible legal rules, like France or Germany.[38] Such rules often include long-fought-for social compromises, such as mandatory codetermination for large corporations to ensure that labor has a voice on companies' boards.[39] By contrast, national law can create challenges for some of the most lucrative strategies for coding capital that involve opting into foreign law to avoid domestic constraints. A recent fad in corporate dealmaking is the use of special-purpose acquisition companies (SPACs), which are corporate vehicles that are established as empty shells that will be filled with assets, typically another company, once a lucrative prospect is identified.[40] They are speculative investment vehicles that conflict with various long-standing corporate-law rules aimed at protecting creditors and minority shareholders, including rules about paid-up capital or limits on the redeemability of shares. Germany, which is known for a rather rigid corporate law, has stifled the development of this market, which is why the only SPACs that are registered on a German stock exchange have been incorporated in Luxembourg.[41] Although some might welcome this legal-arbitrage opportunity, it is not clear why the law should condone speculative practices of this kind that offer lucrative deals to lawyers and financial investors but little else in terms of investment in production. The argument that a country should be able to compete with cutting-edge legal techniques developed in the hubs of global capital, New York or London, serves as a foil for financial speculators and their lawyers, but is not meritorious in substance.

The tendency of choice of law to reduce rather than expand choices for all is not the result of a randomized choice of law; it also cannot be attributed to the true preferences of the parties to a transaction for the legal systems they ended up selecting, because the parties themselves rarely make the choice: their lawyers do.[42] Not even the lawyers know enough legal systems to make a fully informed choice. Instead, they choose the systems they are familiar with, typically the one in which they practice and perhaps another they have encountered in law school.[43] Their clients tend to prefer legal systems that are flexible and have a trajectory of favoring capital over other interests, and on this scale, the common law that is practiced in the United States and the United Kingdom tends to score higher than the civil law.[44]

To guard against a DIY strategy that empowers the rich against the poor, legislatures should place limits on the ease with which economic actors pick and choose from different legal orders or seek to enforce the law of their choice. This is needed to protect the integrity of democratic governance, which means collective self-governance through law, and to protect those who, because of resource constraints, are unable to avail themselves of similar choices. Greater reliance on objective factors for determining the applicable law instead of leaving this to free choice would be a superior solution.[45] For victims of harm caused by accident (tort), many legal systems already rely on objective considerations such as the place where the accident occurred; an example is the EU regulation that harmonized choice-of-law rules for torts.[46] Notably, the European Union allows for deviation from this rule in the case of pollution, the effects of which are often felt far away from where pollutants are emitted. For these cases, member states may grant victims of harm (not just any party) a greater choice over the applicable law.[47] This strikes a careful balance between the legal certainty that objective factors for determining the applicable law offer on the one hand and, on the other, greater flexibility to protect the weaker party. It also complies with the precautionary principle in environmental matters that has been enshrined in EU Treaty law.[48]

Legal arbitrage is conducted primarily through private law, but it deeply affects areas of public law as well, including tax and regulatory law. In fact, these regimes are often the reason why parties revert to private-law legal arbitrage. Most states recognize and enforce most private law, but they do not offer the same courtesy to foreign public law, because this would challenge their sovereignty. In truth, so does the sellout of private law, because it too should reflect the norms of society and not a wish list of capital. Public law is bounded by the territory of the states that enact it. Extending it extraterritorially faces limitations in international law, and enforcing the legal mandates of other states requires treaties between states, such as extradition treaties. Private law, by contrast, has been made portable, and its portability has been vastly increased by the willingness of states to commit their courts to enforcing foreign law without considering whether the rules comply with the norms that govern social and economic relations. Yet private law is just as important for society as state regulation. If private law allows for profit seeking without regard to the costs this imposes on others, it will be difficult to fix this through redistribution. It makes the job of democratically elected legislatures and executives almost impossible because the laws they pass are often avoided by the most powerful players, who freely roam other jurisdictions in search of law that suits their needs. The concept of DIY law includes the ability to exploit differences in fundamental norms, which is a recipe for the further fragmentation of societies and the greater precarity of peoples on the periphery of society.[49] They have a hard time standing up to private power anyhow, but their ability to rely on public power is compromised by legal arbitrage that enables a "transnational liftoff" by the powerful from domestic legal orders.[50]

In theory, anybody can be a legal arbitrageur. Incomplete law, the normative bricolage, and choice-of-law options are equally available to all. In practice, they mostly benefit parties with greater power, resources, and mobility. With sufficient resources, it is possible to hire better lawyers, to persist, and if necessary, to repeat litigation or lobbying efforts, something others can barely afford even once. Litigation is a powerful strategy to bend the law in one's own favor, one case at a time. Persistence has often paid off, even in the case of legal principles that were once deemed "unbending and inveterate."[51] This is how Judge Benjamin Cardozo characterized the duty of loyalty that fiduciaries owe a partner, a beneficiary, or a company and its shareholders. In 1989, Jack Coffee could still write that although much of Delaware's corporate law is enabling and not mandatory, this did not apply to fiduciary duties.[52] But statutory changes on the heels of decades of litigation have allowed companies to opt out of corporate opportunity doctrine (a classic among duty-of-loyalty violations) and made it almost impossible to litigate on the basis of the less demanding duty of care.[53] In addition, for limited partnerships and limited liability companies, fiduciary duties have been made increasingly optional.[54] Given this trajectory, it should not come as a surprise if fiduciary duties eventually become optional for publicly traded corporations.

Mobility is another factor that makes capital the major beneficiary of legal arbitrage. Not every constituency that is affected by law is mobile. Most are not, because they lack the resources or because the law bars them from migrating. Visa requirements and immigration rules restrict the ability of natural persons to cross borders in pursuit of jobs. Labor exploitation has never been recognized as grounds for asylum. Although U.S. law makes undocumented workers who were exploited in the United States eligible for a visa or work authorization, it denies undocumented immigrants back pay if they were unlawfully terminated for their otherwise-protected union organizing, which plays into the hands of their employers.[55] In comparison, corporations are never "undocumented"; they can incorporate anywhere and will be recognized everywhere. The direction of their migration is often to jurisdictions with lower, not higher, labor standards, as the "migration" of corporations globally from North to South in pursuit of weaker labor laws shows.[56] Because employees as well as consumers are structurally vulnerable, Hanoch Dagan and Sagi Peari caution against extending choice of law to these areas of law.[57] Yet the problem of free choice of law, which they endorse in theory as a fundamental principle of liberal law, goes further still. When some exercise their choice of law, others are affected—often those who are not mobile and therefore cannot escape the effects of the choice made by others. A good example is securities regulation. Roberta Romano has argued that free choice should be extended from corporate law to securities law.[58] Investors could vote with their feet by selling stock in companies that make a bad choice. As Merritt Fox has pointed out, however, securities law is not just about investors who trade globally and can easily reallocate their capital; it is also about communities where these companies operate and workers who are not mobile and have few opportunities to relocate to a different jurisdiction.[59] Because of this structural difference, according to Fox, local constituencies, not more mobile actors, should determine the applicable law. More generally, it may be worth considering whether the same choice-of-law principles that are meant to enhance individual freedom should necessarily apply to corporate entities or to financial or other capital assets. They are not freedom fighters, but profit generators. At the very least, a state asked to throw its coercive powers behind the foreign law that privileges these actors or assets should have the option to deny enforcement if enforcement of that law would conflict with the interests of important local constituencies—for instance, labor.[60] This position would be consistent with Dagan and Peari's claim that the freedom to choose one's law "is inherently limited by both interpersonal justice and the parties' compliance with their obligations to support their states' just institutions."[61]

Legal arbitrage results from features of law that are common to all legal systems: law's inherent incompleteness and the coexistence of multiple, often overlapping, legal regimes. Legal arbitrage can therefore be called a core characteristic of capitalist law only if it is structurally biased in favor of capital. The above analysis confirms that it is. Holders of capital command greater resources; they also have the most to gain from exploiting legal-arbitrage opportunities and very little, besides money, to lose. They have access to the best-paid lawyers who know how to design legal-arbitrage strategies to benefit their clients while also claiming that whatever they do is legal. This is most apparent in tax-avoidance strategies. When an international consortium of investigative journalists published the Pandora Papers in 2021, following earlier revelations in the Panama and Paradise Papers, the former U.K. prime minister Tony Blair and many others who had taken advantage of legal tax havens to lower their bills shrugged off the allegation of wrongdoing by insisting that what they had done was legal.[62] So are, by definition, all successful legal-arbitrage strategies: They are designed to be formally compliant with the law while exploiting ambiguities, loopholes, and frictions, even if they violate the law's purpose and the normative foundations of a just social order. And courts have often condoned such practices. Judge Learned Hand, for example, opined that "[a]nyone may so arrange his affairs that his taxes shall be as low as possible; he is not bound to choose that pattern which will best pay the Treasury; there is not even a patriotic duty to increase one's taxes."[63] This is a blanket endorsement of freewheeling egoism and reduces law to a commodity that can be bought and discarded at the behest of private actors. It is anathema to ideas of social justice and to democratic self-governance. Both require a willingness to respect others and their opportunities in life and to play by the rules that are effectively binding on others.

This chapter concludes the analysis of the three features of capitalist law that entrench the priority of private over collective ordering in the legal system. However, when the law becomes a tool in the hands of power players who game it to their own advantage, it is in danger of losing its legitimacy in the eyes of the many and can no longer serve as a normative foundation for a social order based on voluntary compliance with the law.[64] Legal arbitrage, the feature discussed in this chapter, may be the most intractable of the characteristics of capitalist law because it exploits features that are inherent to all law: its indeterminacy and legal plurality. Yet legal arbitrage would not be as powerful a tool for private actors were it not for the willingness of states to embrace private autonomy and outsource their enforcement powers to private actors. Social division is also deepened by the other features of capitalist law that were discussed in the two preceding chapters: the legal empowerment of private actors without effective checks on their power by those who are subject to it and the ease with which such private actors can access the centralized means of coercion to enforce their rights, even when they violate the rights of others. The combination and interaction of these three features have made private law a powerful tool in the hands of resourceful actors. The same features have left many others adrift in a world in which they observe that the law is working for the well-off, but not necessarily for them. The remaining two chapters of the book tackle the question of whether there is a way out: whether capitalist law can be transformed and what it would take to move beyond this regime.

6

Rewiring the System

The analysis in the previous chapters has shown that capitalism is a legal regime that facilitates the appropriation of social resources for private gain and told how it does so. The system has many winners, but even more losers, including people who lack access to the law and resources to meet their own needs and are not able to participate in this system on equal footing. Arguing that there are no alternatives masks the inequities of the current system and the dangers it poses for the values that advocates of capitalism claim for themselves: freedom, autonomy, and self-governance, not just for some but for all. Moreover, the collision course between capitalism and nature pits a social system that is wired to expand at any cost against a naturally bounded system that responds more violently as its limits are challenged. These are the reasons why change is called for, even if it is difficult.

Writing in the 1960s, when the battle between capitalism and socialism was still raging, Andre Gunder Frank argued that overcoming capitalism would require more than reforms designed to make the system more benign at the surface that did not address the underlying structures of inequality and dependence.[1] In his view, the centralization of economic power at the core of the capitalist system, and its employment for extracting surplus from the periphery, constitute the deeper structural features of this regime. The relations between capital and the rest are characterized as relations between center and periphery, and this applies to domestic as well as to global relations. On the geopolitical scale, the former colonies operated as satellites of the metropoles. According to Frank, though many had claimed independence, their dependence on the metropoles continued even after the end of colonial rule. He conceded that considerable change had taken place since, including change in the nature of economic activities conducted at the core as well as on the periphery and change within the institutions that support them. However, in his view, this did not alter the structural dependence of the periphery on the center. "If I have de-emphasized these institutional changes in this essay," he wrote, "it has been to call attention to the essential structural continuity of capitalism and its effects."[2] The logical conclusion from this argument is that the only way out from capitalism, and the dependencies it creates, is to destabilize the global capitalist system through the withdrawal of the peripheral economies. The task of the former colonies, he argued, was to overcome "bourgeois ideology and theory," including "reformist and revisionist policy and opportunism," and instead adopt a "revolutionary Marxist strategy and tactics."[3] Obviously, this has not happened. On the contrary, Soviet-style socialism has collapsed, and most countries that were socialist or embraced at least some of its ideas have converged on the capitalist model. That has contributed to the sense that capitalism is inevitable and has impoverished the search for alternatives not only to capitalism but to socialism as actually practiced.

More recently, the sociologist Joanna Kusiak has suggested that "the overthrow of capitalism (a systemic revolution) is . . . extremely unlikely to occur by means of law."[4] The reason, she argues, is that although law precedes capitalism, it also "plays a constitutive role in its functioning." It operates on the basis of a legal fiction of people as "free" and "equal" subjects, "which performatively masks—as Marx showed—the structural inequality between capital and labour."[5] Still, as the title of her essay suggests, Kusiak also invokes the idea of "trespassing on the law" as a strategy for transformative change. Moreover, in her more recent book *Radically Legal* she shows how law can be employed to chart a path toward social change.[6]

I agree with this. In fact, precisely *because* law is constitutive of capitalism, it must be at the center of change that shall lead beyond this regime.[7] The direction of transformation is difficult to control in the case of complex systems. However, by identifying capitalism's constitutive elements—the way capital is coded in law and the legal features that facilitate its reconstitution—it is possible to pinpoint vulnerabilities within the system that could be exploited for change. At the very least, the existing system can be disrupted. This will increase uncertainty, at least in the short term, but also encourage experimentation with alternative institutions. Stability may not be immediately within reach, but in light of the increasing volatility of the political and ecological environment, the existing system offers little consolation. In fact, a lot of bottom-up innovation in the legal organization of political and economic relations is already under way, indicating the urge to find alternatives to a system that is perceived by many as unjust and unsustainable.

Crises are often feared, and for good reason. They are steeped in uncertainty, and there is no guarantee that the system will restabilize instead of further destabilizing, which might produce more violence and suffering than positive change. Still, crises can and often do bring about *transformative* change. The Greek verb *krínein,* from which the word *crisis* derives, means to judge or decide.[8] A crisis, then, is not just a state of unrest and uncertainty but a time and space for solving problems and finding solutions that promise a better future. Crises often bring about change, not by wiping out the past, but by facilitating the recombination of what was with something new. As John Padgett noted, "Invention never eliminates the past; it rewires it."[9] In calmer times, complex systems tend to reconstitute themselves because known practices promise future stability. The fact that these very practices are contributing to the destabilization of the system by eroding social cohesion is often overlooked, which is why violent disruptions are rarely predicted and their causes become clear only in hindsight. Still, the search for new solutions can produce "new life forms," even if only as the unintentional "byproducts" of a crisis.[10]

Historical transformations often occur in the midst of prolonged crises that can span years, decades, or centuries. Padgett uses the example of the Netherlands, which emerged from the convulsions of war with Spain, internal civil strife, and religious conflict in the period between 1560 and 1610 to enter its gilded age. Looking back, we can now say that this was when capitalism emerged. He shows that the transformation owed much to parallel institutional change in different parts of the social system, all geared toward a common enemy and the nature of its rules: centralized rule by the Spanish king, which demanded subordination politically, economically, and religiously. Within half a century, a very different system emerged: overlapping federalist structures in the economy, in government, and in religious life.[11] As a side effect, this transformation brought about organizational innovations, among them the modern business corporation. Its core features were first developed for the Dutch East India Company, a colonial enterprise that was chartered by the Dutch Republic and funded primarily by merchants.[12] It operated as a vehicle for controlling the trade routes to the Far East and for generating profits for its shareholders. Its original charter still had many features in common with the trading companies that preceded it, including a limited life span and the right of shareholders to eventually retrieve their capital contribution— after ten years rather than after each journey. However, when the ten years were up, the charter was amended to make capital contributions permanent. This capital lock-in became central to the evolution of large business corporations with publicly traded shares and an indefinite life span—the very institutions that today operate as private government over others.[13] The prolonged crises that preceded the Dutch gilded age facilitated institutional innovations that transformed the existing system. Institutional change altered behavior and, critically, expectations about the behavior of others. Once new patterns formed and replaced the uncertainty that is an inevitable part of a search process, change became institutionalized.

Today, capitalism finds itself in a prolonged state of crisis. The "great financial crisis" of 2008 was only its most visible manifestation. That crisis had been decades in the making and is still lingering today.[14] Moreover, the great financial crisis was followed by several smaller financial crises and eventually by the Covid pandemic. Many have described the world today as being in "multi-crises," the most visible signs of which are inequality, social divisiveness, climate change, and pandemics.[15] So far, these crises have largely been kept under control thanks to massive interventions by governments and central banks in the heartland of capitalism: the United States, the United Kingdom, the European Union, and Japan. Their efforts prevented a meltdown but did not bring about lasting stability. In fact, the continuing fragility of global financial capitalism has made it increasingly reliant on life support that only the best-resourced states can offer.[16]

The elites in the countries at the core of global capitalism have, of course, the greatest interest in maintaining the system, and their support for government interventions is best understood as an attempt to bring it back to where it was thought to have been before the crisis. However, the support the governments of these countries offered, especially to the financial system, proved to be difficult to unwind, which is not surprising. After all, had the system been stable, the crisis should not have occurred, and if the crisis had been only a blip in an otherwise stable system, the system could have fixed itself. Instead, continuous liquidity support for the financial system has been normalized. By demonstrating their willingness to provide additional liquidity whenever needed irrespective of a legal right to access liquidity, the leading central banks have underwritten the entire financial system, including the shadow banking system.[17] As a result, the costs of finance have effectively been socialized, and the facade of separate spheres of money and finance, the former managed by public agents, the latter left to free markets, has crumbled.[18] There is hardly a better example of the state being caught in its own trap.[19]

Not everyone may have fully recognized the implications of this state of the world. It is more convenient to stick to worldviews and explanations that validate existing beliefs. However, growing calls for central banks to place more weight on inequality or on greening the economy by selecting the assets against which they lend with an eye on ecological sustainability, suggest a greater awareness of how deeply central bank policy penetrates not just the financial system but all of society as well as the environment. If additional proof of the importance of social resources for the survival of capitalism was needed, it came in the response to the Covid pandemic. Once again, central banks intervened to stabilize the system, but this time around, broader support from governments, including through legislative action, was extended to non-financial firms, small businesses, and households.[20] The state demonstrated that it had the capacity to provide for most of its people—at least some states did. One of the lasting lessons of both the great financial crisis and the Covid pandemic is that center-periphery relations cut deep and hinder the ability of governments in countries on the periphery to protect their people. These countries often lack full monetary sovereignty to expand the money supply, and they do not have access to vaccines and other medications because they are behind a paywall built on patents.[21] Countries in the global North could have extended additional help. They could have provided swap lines to the central banks of countries on the periphery to ensure that those central banks had access to the dollar, and they could have waived the patent protection of lifesaving Covid vaccines to enable the legal production of generic drugs or mandate licenses to produce the patented ones.[22] Instead, states in the so-called advanced economies hid behind the need to protect private intellectual-property rights and their central banks' mandate to protect price stability domestically, not globally. The central banks themselves retreated to their old monetarist positions as soon as inflation raised its head again. They turned to interest-rate hikes as their trusted tool for cooling the economy, even though it was far from clear that the root causes of inflation had much to do with excessively high wages or loose credit conditions.[23] It is, however, notable that this knee-jerk reaction of central banks came under substantial critique from economists who challenged the assertion that inflation is always and inevitably a monetary phenomenon, as Milton Friedman had asserted.[24] Alternative responses, such as price caps, were put on the table to address energy shortages caused by war (Russia's invasion of Ukraine) and Covid-induced ruptures of global supply chains.[25] It is too early to tell which side is winning in the theoretical debate, but a profound challenge to monetary orthodoxy, which for decades has strangled the imagination of policymakers and academics alike, can be taken as a sign of an opening.

The dissatisfaction with real existing capitalism is becoming palpable. The most visible sign of this is the "populist" movement, which has propelled into office in several countries, including old democracies, new leaders who are openly hostile to constitutional constraints and the norms they are built on and ready to shake up a system that many believe no longer serves them.[26] The various movements that are often branded as "populist" may not agree on much, but one message is coming through loudly and clearly: The people no longer accept the notion that there is "no alternative" to the existing system.[27] They may not blame capitalism; indeed, many might blame "the state" or "the elites" instead, or worse, put the blame on the weakest of all: migrants, the undocumented, and the stateless. The world has been here before. At the beginning of the twentieth century, a great reversal upended political and economic stability, as those left behind or whose lives had been turned upside down by war and its aftershocks looked to communism or fascism as harbingers of a better world.[28] This is not to say that extreme outcomes such as these are inevitable. But if left unattended, the unfolding dynamics of disaffection and distrust of the existing regime may precipitate a crisis that would be difficult to control.

Indeed, it seems that conditions are ripe for transformative change. The question is whether these conditions can be harnessed for moving beyond a system that, by its own logic, deepens inequality and social divisiveness and recklessly destroys the environment, even in the face of a deepening climate crisis. One might hope that different strands of change will align just as they did in the Netherlands at the cusp of capitalism's takeoff, only in a different direction. Things are more complicated today, not least because capitalism not only is deeply embedded in economic and political relations; it is a legal regime. Capitalism has been hardwired into our economic and political systems through law, which makes it difficult to topple the systems without destroying the foundations of social order. And law's tendency to preserve works largely against and not for change. But it also follows that changing the wiring may well change the system.

Identifying law as a harbinger of change differs from conventional Marxist accounts that emphasize instead the need for altering the materialist conditions as a precondition for overcoming capitalism. However, if law is understood as constitutive of capitalism, the distinction between materialist conditions, on the one hand, and institutions, on the other, becomes blurred.[29] As noted earlier, it is not land as nature or machines as engineering achievements but the right to a plot of land or to the innovation that created the blueprint for the machine that vests the rightful owner with the ability to capture its pecuniary value. Put differently, capitalism derives its adaptability and longevity not from physical power and control, but from deploying critical *social* resources for private wealth creation: the law, including the state's coercive powers, and the monetary system.

Capitalism's initial rise coincided with the enclosure and privatization of land. Only when land can be sold and mortgaged can owners realize land's expected future value today. The same techniques—the legal enclosure of assets, the vesting of title to only a few, and the socializing of risk associated with their use—were subsequently applied to other objects and claims, and also to knowledge and data. Intangible assets, such as financial claims and intellectual-property rights, owe their very existence to law. Debt is an obligation between two persons whereby one lends something (money or goods) to another who promises to return it, or an equivalent, in the future.[30] Turning debt into capital required legal change that made debt fungible almost on par with money.[31] Credit is private money and is joined at the hip to state money because private money is denominated in public money and holders of private money expect that they will be able to convert that private money into state money on demand.[32] The privatization of social resources has not stopped at money, but extends to knowledge and culture. Patents, copyrights, and trademarks are legal devices that create monopolies. Absent these devices, anybody would have access to the knowledge, innovation, skills, or artwork that humans have created. Because they are non-rivalrous, use or consumption of them by some would not take away anything from others. If some are given the privilege to monopolize them, it is only because the law empowers them to do so. Data is yet another example. Information about individuals and social groups is produced as a byproduct of their lives. When information technology made it possible to capture behavior at scale and place it on a device, tech companies, as owners of these devices, first secured de facto control over it, but they did not stop there.[33] They lobbied legislatures to recognize their physical control as legal, and they rely on trade-secret law and, critically, the absence of effective legal protection of the rights of data creators.

As these examples suggest, capital is made in law, and capitalism—the system—lives and thrives on the capacity of the system to expand by coding ever more assets as capital and by employing the authority of the law and the state's means of coercion to protect those assets. The evolution of capitalism has been marked by continuity and change.[34] As noted, Frank saw continuity in the deep structural divide between the (colonial) metropolis and its satellites, not in the institutions that organize these relations, because they appeared to be too malleable for explaining the persistence of structural hierarchies over time. By contrast, I argue that legal institutions are at the very heart of the structural divide between the center and the periphery, and the haves and have-nots. The adaptability of law to new technological and economic developments allows it to project authority and thereby stabilize future expectations even when the nature of economic activities or assets changes. How law does this is important to understand because only then will it be possible to pinpoint the most critical aspects of the law that require rewiring in order to change the system.

Some of the answers to this question can be found in Niklas Luhmann's analysis of law as a social system.[35] His attempt to explain law as an autopoietic, or self-referential and actorless, system may be less relevant for this point.[36] Much of his account of the evolution of law remains valid without these aspects, like the idea that law operates according to a logic that is distinct from either politics or economics. The function of law is to stabilize normative expectations, not regarding what exactly people will do—an impossible task—but about what happens when their behavior deviates from expectations. By sanctioning deviant behavior, either in criminal law or by giving private actors the right to sue for damages or obtain an injunction, the law creates normative expectations that help stabilize social relations. Only the law determines what is legal or illegal, writes Luhmann, and it does so in accordance with "valid" norms.[37] Ultimately, the final decisions over these matters are made by courts, which, at least in principle, are bound by law, not by changing political or economic sentiments. Importantly, the validity of norms can change over time, even without formal legal change, through "the ongoing reproduction of the difference between variation and selection."[38] Critical are the selection criteria, including the normative principles that inform them. Many laws that had normative force in the past fell into disuse and were eventually overturned by formal legal change.

One might dismiss this as an example of powerful lobbies leaning on courts or legislatures to get their way. Such direct influence is not uncommon, but it corrupts the law and diminishes its ability to stabilize expectations, since decisions would become arbitrary and more difficult to predict. In fact, legal evolution within capitalism has for the most part been more sophisticated than that. Legal change can be achieved by packaging novel claims or arguments in ways that are consistent with the internal logic of the legal system but reflect different normative aspirations. "Interests have to be presented for the legal system and its operations in such a way that they make reasoned decisions possible," writes Luhmann.[39] Also, this preparation typically involves an interpretation of law that is close enough to established legal principles for the judge to buy into, even as it moves the needle incrementally in a new direction.[40] As Luhmann notes, the law can therefore aptly be described as a "historical machine"; it produces change by filtering social change into legal categories that help stabilize expectations around it.

For Luhmann, these processes operate largely independently of politics and economics, although he recognized that these three social systems intersect with one another. My analysis of capitalism as a legal regime suggests a much closer relation between these systems, because the law affects behavior not only by stabilizing expectations but by providing the resource with which assets are coded as capital. For a social or economic interest to become legally relevant, it must be translated into legal categories. This is how the legal system can be strategically employed to allow economic interests to control politics and, through it, legal change. An example of this coupling between law, economics, and politics is contract law. As Luhmann put it, "The audacity of this form [contract] does not reveal itself until it is realized that through it the legal system and, as far as the use of physical force is concerned, the political system, can be conditioned by the private sector, that is, the economic system."[41]

Viewed in this light, contract law, seemingly the most innocent of all institutions of private law because it is based on voluntarism and mutual consent, is the vehicle by which powerful economic interests can capture the state. Courts are programmed to enforce these interests as long as they are presented in the appropriate legal form. In this way, without realizing it, courts can become the agents of economic interests that confer on them the aura of legality and the power of enforceability.

In theory, legislation could be the great equalizer and correct imbalances that result from litigation and the case law it produces, and in some areas and in some periods it has played that role. Often cited for this principle is the wave of New Deal legislation in the United States in the 1930s. This legislation—including laws aimed at stabilizing the financial system, such as the Securities Act and the Securities and Exchange Act, which established a regulatory regime for securities markets, as well as the Glass-Steagall Act, which separated investment from commercial banks; but also the Fair Labor Standards Act, which created a minimum wage; the National Labor Relations Act, which affirmed the right to organize; the National Housing Act, which safeguarded homeowners from foreclosure; and the Social Security Act, which provided a source of income to retirees and the unemployed, among others—aimed to restore the balance between the working class and the upper class, which had been decimated by the Great Depression. The combined force of all these laws did usher in a new era, validating Padgett's findings that change is likely to be transformative when it occurs in parallel in multiple domains of social life. Finance, housing, labor, and social security constituted one package.

The reforms' Achilles' heel, however, was that they did not alter private law and its normative foundations. Private actors supported by sophisticated lawyers soon began to dismantle the New Deal by using private law to avoid its reach. They outsourced labor to avoid the reach of labor legislation back home and developed new financial instruments, including derivatives, to escape new financial regulation and capital controls. Over time they became bolder and mobilized the courts and lobbied legislatures to roll back parts of the New Deal, including financial regulation that was designed to enhance financial stability. The process of rolling back the New Deal may be viewed as capture of government by private actors. This conclusion cannot be completely refuted. However, Luhmann's analysis adds an important aspect to this simple story of capture. In his view, legislation that expresses the social will increases variety in a system, opening the system to new influences including interests that seek to exploit uncertainty for their own ends. Routine operations that rely on well-known, or redundant, information are overwhelmed by new facts and new interpretations—the kind of disruption and uncertainty that is likely to usher in change. In the law, Luhmann explains, greater variety registers as noise, at least in the short term. Courts will have to exercise more discretion and issue more ad hoc rulings because noise makes it difficult to achieve internal consistency of the law. The increase in variety, even without adding ideology or outright capture through lobbying or forum shopping, renders the routine functioning of the legal system illusionary.

This analysis leaves us with a conundrum. On one hand, the interplay of law, politics, and the economy can lead to the domination of economic interests over politics through law; on the other, legislation as an expression of pluralistic politics by legal means forces courts to abandon consistency and unity, which leaves them with more discretion not less, and which in turn undermines democratic self-governance. Several paths might lead out of this conundrum. The legal system might lose its relevance as a critical ordering device in pluralist, complex societies. For an interim period, the law might still serve as a tool in the hands of powerful economic interests, but this may not last, because law will inevitably lose its capacity to stabilize normative expectations. More people will opt out or take the law into their own hands by devising their own subsystems of rules. As a result, the legal system might disintegrate.

But what might replace it? One answer is anarchy. Another is the digital code, as reflected in the notion that "code is law."[42] Versions of both are already upon us. In many parts of the world, formal law has never played an integrative role as a stabilizer of expectations and has divided rather than united the people. This is true in particular for the former colonies where the law that was imposed from the outside was and continues to be regarded by many as alien and contrary to strongly held communal beliefs.[43] A symptom of this state of affairs is deeply ingrained corruption, but the strongest manifestation of the absence of normative stabilizers is the phenomenon of "failed states."[44]

But perhaps it is too early to give up on law quite yet. Although the dismal projections just mentioned should not be easily dismissed, especially when adding the stress of climate change to political challenges that legal orders face today, there may still be a different way of configuring the legal system—rewiring it. This approach recognizes that complex systems require scalable systems of ordering, but also that the legal coding of socioeconomic relations has reached a level of complexity domestically as well as globally that cannot simply be undone. The legal entanglements are too complex and the interests that support them too powerful. Instead, law needs to be rewired from within. As in all major social transformations, this will entail combining new ways of doing things with what has come before. There is no guarantee that transformative change will occur fast enough to escape the darker alternatives suggested. Neither is there a guarantee that it will lead in a direction that is normatively desirable. No change, however, is not an option, because change, which the multiple crises are a symptom of, is already upon us. The major question is whether change can be channeled to support freedom and dignity for all within diversity. This requires a fundamental normative reorientation, especially of private law, with greater respect for the rights of others; it requires nothing less than the democratization of private law.

7

Beyond Capitalist Law

Capitalism is a regime that has been forged from law, but not just any law. Capitalist law is characterized by the relative autonomy that private law enjoys from public law, and from public law's normative foundations, which have been enshrined in constitutions. Public law evolved together with the consolidation of central power and its subsequent differentiation into the regulatory and the welfare states. Private law allows for a more rapid adaptation of law to a changing environment than could be achieved through lengthy processes of legislation. Political control is more easily exerted over public law than private law because the implementation and enforcement of public law lies in the hands of public agents, whereas it lies with private agents in the case of private law. Different normative ideas animate the two bodies of law: collective self-governance with constraints on executive power as well as majoritarian overreach in the case of public law, and individual autonomy and freedom in the case of private law. Herein lies the "antithesis" of private and public law, which Pashukanis identified as foundational for capitalist law.

Public law has allowed the state to expand its reach and has facilitated the rise of the regulatory state as well as the welfare state. Often overlooked is the extent to which public law has also enabled and spurred economic development. The best example may well be the financial system. State-issued money and financial markets are joined at the hip. The state has franchised to the private sector the money-creation process but backstops the system to avoid major calamities. This means that financial intermediaries benefit from a relatively soft budget constraint, even though private actors are supposed to operate under a hard survival constraint in a competitive market.¹ This is why the survival of banks, and increasingly other financial intermediaries, is not dependent just on what they do but also on what the state is willing to do for them as a way to safeguard the financial system.² To protect the system and society against its inherent fragility, the state has also regulated the financial system, but only partly and without seriously curtailing its profitability to private operators, even as they put the system at risk. This is evidenced by the large and growing "shadow banking sector"—the practice of banking outside regulated banks.³ Over a decade after the great financial crisis of 2008 and the reforms that were meant to re-regulate the system, shadow banking is larger today than it has ever been. It is now engulfing, even threatening, bank-based financial systems.⁴

All of this has been possible within political systems that are organized democratically and in which public power is justified and constrained by a constitution. Most constitutions in force today embrace fundamental civil and political rights and include provisions that are aimed at holding public power to account. Increasingly, though, these mechanisms have been weakened by attempts to insulate much of the private sector, including financial markets, from democratic control. Oversight of these markets has been delegated to independent courts, independent regulators, and independent central banks. Independence is supposed to help insulate these institutions from executive and legislative overreach, but it can also make them the targets of capture by private interests at the expense of collective interests. Further, the more democratic controls are kept at bay, the more states morph into technocracies that ensure the operation of a system that works primarily for capital while keeping the majority of the people away from the levers of power.

Private law has been largely outsourced to the private sector—to individuals and entities that use it to organize their affairs in the shadow of the state's enforcement powers. It predates the evolution of the modern state and democratic constitutionalism, but its core tenets, contract and property rights as well as corporate law, have been augmented by state power. Contrary to conventional wisdom, contracts are only rarely expressions of bargains that reflect reciprocal rights and obligations of the parties to the contract. More often they are instruments of control by the party that dictates the terms of the contract over others who, for lack of other options, are subject to that party's private rule. Property has long ceased to be primarily about individual use and control of an object; its primary function in capitalism is the control over future cash flows and the ability to realize them here and now. And it is no accident that corporations were born in the age of colonialism, when they served the dual function of conquest and profit. Today, they may no longer be explicitly authorized to rule over people, but their command over the assets they own and the power to impose contracts on others comes close to it. Further, constitutions as well as international treaties protect investors not just against outright expropriation but against any interference of some significance with the expectation of monetary rewards, and in this way subordinate the will of democratic polities to investors' demands.

By legally empowering private actors, granting them access to the coercive powers of the state, and endorsing expansive legal arbitrage, private law has served as a tool for creating bastions of private power that lack the kinds of constraints that have operated as checks on public power. The task then is to rein in the scale and scope of economic power. Since this power is owed in large measure to law, in particular to private law, its reconfiguration must start here.

Private-law theorists have long wrestled with the question of how power that is conferred by law on private parties may be justified. Whereas to many economists the most important question is whether a transaction is efficient in the sense that it allocates an asset to whoever makes the best use of it, legal theorists are more likely to ask whether the allocation of rights and the power they confer can be justified in normative terms.[5]

This question is particularly pertinent in the case of property rights, which give owners (nearly) absolute control over a resource, including the power to deny others access to and the use of that resource.[6] Blackstone's characterization of property rights as a "despotic dominion" has always been an exaggeration. The rights of owners are inherently constrained by the rights of neighbors and by the victims of tort actions emanating from the property, and they can be further curtailed by contract or statutory law, including zoning rules, for example.[7] And contract law can confer substantial power on non-owners, such as creditors. From an economic perspective, this is not troublesome, because it reflects the normal operation of the market mechanism. Whoever can offer terms the other party cannot trump or resist, should get the deal.

But this is not the only way to think about contract law, as Martijn Hesselink has shown.[8] It is equally possible to think about binding contracts, or private law in general, from a democratic point of view. "It is difficult to see why a person ought to accept living under laws made by others," Hesselink writes, adding that there is no principled difference between "criminal law, tax law, or any other branch of law."[9] He rejects the idea that private law should be understood as a sphere in which persons encounter each other just as persons rather than as citizens or members of a polity.[10] To him, all are always and necessarily part of a community, and their rights must be construed and weighed in relation to that community. The slogan "no taxation without representation" of the Boston Tea Party back in 1773 could thus be restated as "no binding commitment without actual consent"—where "actual" means a substantive voluntary agreement as opposed to a volitional act when no viable alternatives are present.[11]

Hesselink argues persuasively that private law as configured in capitalist regimes does not meet fundamental principles of justice, whether social (distributional) or interpersonal (relational) justice. Within this system, he suggests, *social* inequality is "reproduced and exacerbated" as *interpersonal* inequality. The experienced reality is domination by a few over the rest and in large measure through law, which contributes to the erosion of democracy because it undermines collective self-governance: "In other words, rising inequality and the erosion of democracy are two sides of the same coin. And this coin could not be minted without private law."[12]

To rectify this situation, he proposes a progressive private-law code for Europe (EPL-code), but this idea could be extended to other jurisdictions as well. The EPL-code is not meant as yet another attempt at codifying European private law, an effort that has failed in the past.[13] Instead, its goal is to promulgate *normative principles of justice* for private law at the EU level. These principles could eventually be incorporated in EU Treaty law and the constitutions of its member states. Hesselink does not specify the principles he has in mind, arguing instead that this should be left to public deliberation. The broader goal of the EPL-code would be to ensure that "private law works for all." To achieve this goal, he suggests, we must give proper consideration to "the actual characteristics of the parties" and "the real circumstances in which they conclude their private transactions."[14] Some claims that currently find support in the law on purely formalistic grounds (like the enforcement of contracts that lack actual consent) would lose legal support, whereas others that lack support (such as more participatory rights of workers) might be recognized and protected in the future. In effect, Hesselink argues for a reset of the normative expectations of private law—of the rights it condones and the actions it deems enforceable.

A new normative foundation of private law that aligns it with the normative foundations of democratic constitutionalism may have adverse consequences, which are important to spell out and weigh against the advantages such a push might produce. Adherents of a formal construction of law, who identify justice with internal consistency and prioritize the independence of law from external influence, frequently warn against introducing moral or ethical principles into the operation of the law. Luhmann, for example, argued that only by keeping morals out of individual legal judgments can we assess the legal system itself on moral grounds.[15] As discussed earlier, he assumed a high degree of autonomy of the law from other social systems. If, instead, one takes the view that law is not and cannot be autonomous from the political, economic, social, or indeed the moral and ethical forces that shape it, the argument loses much of its force. It is not clear what is gained by assessing the legal system as such on moral grounds while being agnostic about the morality of specific applications of the law, which in turn shape the future evolution of the law. Adding morals may add additional noise to the process of finding legal solutions because there is likely to be disagreement about what this means on a case-by-case basis. But that is exactly why enshrining normative principles in a code (preferably a binding one) would be helpful. It would focus deliberations on principles whose meaning may be contested, but it would be much more difficult to substitute economic efficiency for social justice.

Moreover, given that a formalistic legal system that has largely avoided introducing matters of justice into private law has been used as a tool for promoting economic injustice and private government without effective accountability, it is difficult to find a good reason for keeping morals at bay. Instead, only by infusing private law with principles of justice can we counter the injustice that the system currently produces. Luhmann concedes as much when he suggests that, from the perspective of legal theory, one might bemoan the use of law for social policy because it leads to the "decay of specific legal rationality." From a sociological point of view, however, one might argue that "it puts responsiveness to socially prevalent and changing preferences in the place of what is traditionally called justice."[16] In short, it would enable a shift from formal to substantive justice, a shift that is long overdue.

Whether a soft code is the right starting point for such far-reaching change, as Hesselink proposed, however, is a different question. Perhaps more cannot be achieved at this point given the likely opposition of the business community and their lawyers to any attempt to move further. A soft code might send a powerful signal about the aspiration for change, but it also could serve as an argument that the matter has been settled. That would be self-defeating because, in the end, lasting change can be achieved only if deliberations about justice become part of the legal discourse not just in general terms but also when the actual enforcement of rights and obligations is at stake. Moreover, real change should not stop at substantive law and would have to include civil-procedure rules, which govern access to the court and to the consolidated means of coercion—they determine who will have standing and on what grounds one may bring a case. In short, a soft EPL-code may be necessary as a first step, but it should be followed by binding commitments.

The transformation and democratization of private law should be grounded in substantive principles of justice that are broadly supported in society. It should be complemented by rules that would allow victims of injustice to break through restrictions in contracts that prevent them from litigating their cases, at least when important questions of justice are involved. Whether we can rely on courts alone, and whether the current organization of the court system would be up to the task, is questionable. One could imagine complementary citizen tribunals, akin to juries, that are tasked with addressing important normative questions that often arise in the course of litigation and that stretch the role of judges as adjudicators to include legislation.[17] Many cases that are litigated raise novel normative issues that should be decided by legislatures, but it often takes years for them to respond to social or technological change.[18] Meanwhile, courts remain the go-to institutions to determine how old law is applied to new facts, which plays into the hands of the more resourceful players.

A good example is the status of drivers for car services such as Uber and Lyft—whether they are employees of these companies, and therefore entitled to receive worker benefits, or self-employed, which ensures that they carry the entire risk of their jobs themselves. Courts, legislatures, and citizens acting through referenda have come out differently on this matter. The critical normative question is who should be charged with making such a decision when existing law offers little guidance for new cases that arise in substantially different circumstances. Common-law courts, which are officially credited with lawmaking powers, have long argued that they do not create new law but instead find legal solutions to new cases in established legal principles. As the pace of social, as well as technological, change increases, however, this argument becomes less compelling. New challenges call for new solutions, which often require a reassessment of the normative issues at stake. Oftentimes litigation reveals the need for change, and one of the advantages of case law is that the law can be adapted in real time, whereas legislation might take years, if not decades. Yet at issue in these cases are often political and normative, not just legal, questions, which call for democratic decision-making processes.

If one were to develop a just private-law code (JPL) not just for the European Union but for legal systems throughout the globe, the first challenge would be to determine the principles that should go into it. The choice could be left to "the people"—as Hesselink suggests. In this sense, the JPL would be a much overdue update to the social contract that produced democratic constitutions, which in turn established the principles for holding public power to account and endorsed individual civil and political rights as bulwarks against the state. These social contracts were, of course, fictions. As a general rule, constitutions were not created in public but in deliberations among a select group of people, often referred to as the fathers (and sometimes mothers) of the constitution. Perhaps one could do better today with modern information technology or recruit a group of truly representative citizens to develop the principles for the JPL in line with ideas for "lottocracies."[19] Still, asking the people or a cross section of them to start from scratch in developing the normative foundations for private law might be a tall order, especially given the fact that private law has been largely shielded from public scrutiny and remains obscure to most. It has been naturalized as the bedrock of the economy and as something that ought not to be touched, perhaps only regulated at the margins. This makes it difficult to even draw public attention to private law as a target of social struggle.

Given these challenges, I propose to launch a debate about the future of private law by spelling out the normative foundations that might govern it. A useful starting point, I suggest, is the "human capabilities" approach, jointly developed by Amartya Sen and Martha Nussbaum.[20] I do not mean to rule out other approaches that may be equally or more promising for the democratization of private law, and I invite others to join the debate about the best approach. There are, however, good reasons why this approach might be a hopeful starting point for transformative change. One reason, perhaps counterintuitively, is that the capabilities approach shares many similarities with the classic canon of human rights that has influenced legal and political systems in the West and elsewhere. This has both advantages and disadvantages. On the plus side, relative familiarity may expand the number of supporters, who may find it less threatening than more radical approaches that depart from these foundations.[21] On the negative side, the proximity to individual rights may signal yet another Western-centrist approach that ignores cultural diversity and has too often failed to achieve its normative promises in the past.[22] In my view, the pros outweigh the cons, especially when the capabilities approach is not regarded as the end but the beginning of a deliberative process that seeks to establish a new normative baseline for economic relations.

At the center of the *human* capabilities approach is the human being, not an abstract person that is defined by legal rights, and certainly not the corporation or similar legal person. This already sets the capabilities approach apart from the traditional rights-based approach because, as we have seen, that rights-based approach has allowed corporations to claim many human rights for themselves and even use these legal empowerments against humans. For practical reasons it may be useful to allow corporations and other business organizations to act as property owners and to contract in their own name, but this does not need to also entail constitutional protections of their rights on par with humans.

Amartya Sen developed the capabilities approach as a critique of the field of economics. Economics, he suggested, does not consider the human condition and thereby fails to achieve its own goals.[23] The discipline is primarily "concerned with the relation between commodities and people," including how commodities are made and in what quantities, what their qualities might be, and "what people get out of commodities."[24] This thinking is not only ingrained in economics but also, as we have seen, deeply ingrained in the commodity form of law (Pashukanis). Questions of justice, Sen suggested, cannot be answered in any meaningful way unless there is some understanding about "how a person's interests may be judged and his or her personal 'state' assessed." Concerning this, economics has little, if anything, to say. Instead, it has satisfied itself with the idea of "utility." As a result, human beings have been reduced to "rational fools, who are unable to distinguish between perfectly distinguishable questions about one's happiness, one's desire, one's view of one's own welfare, one's motivation, one's maximand in choice behavior, and so on."[25] Instead of focusing on utility, Sen argued, the emphasis should be on "the *real* opportunity that a person has especially compared with others."[26] In his rendering of the capabilities approach, opportunities mean "functionings," not utility.[27] Expanding the "capabilities" of persons enables them to lead the kind of lives they value, and have reason to do so.[28]

Martha Nussbaum has taken a somewhat different approach. She also starts from the individual human being, "the ultimate subject of justice."[29] To her, capabilities are also about outcomes, but she downplays the importance of functioning and instead emphasizes human flourishing.[30] And although she suggests that capabilities are a "subspecies" of individual rights, she insists that the capabilities approach departs from a rights-based framework that has left too many blind spots where injustice breeds. Individual rights, she reminds us, tend to be framed as negative rights against the *state*. Positive rights, which capabilities are a subspecies of, are eyed with skepticism because they require more from the state than merely abstaining from the infringements of rights; the state must take positive actions to provide individuals with the means for realizing rights to housing, food, or health care, for example.

This rights framing, according to Nussbaum, too narrowly focuses on the state and underestimates the state's capacity to proactively support its people, which is better captured by the capabilities approach. She points out that countries like India and South Africa have developed a robust history of positive-rights adjudication, which demonstrates the capacity of the state and its legal system to handle the demands inherent to positive rights.[31] However, she also argues that "the rights language is strongly linked with the traditional distinction between a public sphere, which the state may regulate, and a private sphere, which it must leave alone."[32] This has resulted in, among other things, a neglect of women's rights because the family was long designated as private, which left women, children, and household animals at the mercy of the male head of the family.[33]

More generally, separating the public from the private and limiting fundamental rights to rights against the state has enabled the rise of private power in capitalism, as discussed in this book. Centering the discussion on human capabilities clarifies that what is at stake is not "just" a claim to be left alone that is directed against the state, but a normative commitment about the respect that humans owe one another, whether they act in their own capacity as individuals, through associations or business organizations, or, in fact, through their political agents. The capabilities approach denies the "right" to do as one pleases irrespective of the consequences this might have for others, and it demands that society actively create the conditions within which a life that one has reason to value is attainable for all.

Capabilities are innate to every human being (and according to Nussbaum, also to nonhuman animals), irrespective of one's place of birth or citizenship.[34] They do not require membership in a political community or citizenship of a state. In this sense, capabilities do not require a "right to have rights," in the words of Hannah Arendt; they are entitlements at birth against the world. The obligation to realize them lies with all of humanity, which, in the words of Nussbaum, "is under a collective obligation to find ways of living and cooperating together so that all human beings have decent lives."[35] This may sound utopian given the current state of the world, but, I would argue, there is truly no alternative.

Normatively and conceptually, Nussbaum's rendering of the capabilities approach offers a framework for assessing the state of the world from both a social- and a relational-justice perspective and points to a different future than capitalism, a system in which we are trapped. She has also gone a step further and specified a list of capabilities the realization of which should be the guideline for any just society or just legal system. It is not a definitive list, but meant as the basis for future deliberations, and she is mindful of the need to adapt it to cultural differences and preferences as long as those preferences do not undermine the rights of all to live in dignity. The human capabilities she identified include (1) life; (2) bodily health; (3) bodily integrity;

(4) senses, imagination, and thought; (5) emotions; (6) practical reason; (7) affiliation; (8) other species, in particular nonhuman animals; (9) play; and (10) material and political control over one's environment.[36] Each is described in general terms to leave room for different specifications.

As can be seen, quite a few capabilities have counterparts in the canon of civil and political rights. However, there are also important departures in the ways the capabilities have been framed. A good example is the capability of having control over one's environment.[37] In Nussbaum's conception, this capability has two components, one political, the other material. The first stands for "[b]eing able to participate effectively in political choices that govern one's life; having the right of political participation, [and] protections of free speech and association."[38] The second encompasses "[b]eing able to hold property (both land and movable goods), and having property rights on an equal basis with others; having the right to seek employment on an equal basis with others; and having the freedom from unwarranted search and seizure. In work, being able to work as a human."[39]

In effect, Nussbaum establishes normative equivalence between political participation and economic prosperity, and between property and work, implying that these different manifestations of social control should be treated equally and with the same respect, and should arguably be afforded equal legal protections. In short, private law and individual rights are not a license to disregard others; the power they confer entails obligations for ensuring that others too have the capability to lead lives they have reason to value.

Translating theory into principles for a JPL that might change the operation of law to advance human capabilities is, of course, a major challenge. It is not possible to develop a detailed road map within the remaining pages of this book. But it is possible to identify pathways and possible dead ends as one searches for ways to operationalize the normative aspiration of the capabilities approach.

The simplest strategy would be to use this approach as a bright-line rule against harming others, but this has little promise, as suggested by the fate of the Global Compact. It endorses ten principles for global businesses derived from international law, which businesses are asked to adhere to on a voluntary basis.[40] "Businesses should support and respect the protection of internationally proclaimed human rights," reads the first; "[b]usinesses should uphold the freedom of association and the effective recognition of the right to collective bargaining," the fourth; and "[b]usinesses should support a precautionary approach to environmental challenges," the seventh. There is no requirement for businesses to sign the compact, and few repercussions await those that do but fail to live up to the principles they formally endorsed. Nor does the compact empower individuals, labor, or environmental advocates to hold businesses to account other than by trying to shame them.

A JPL should go further and offer guidance to judges or citizen tribunals for applying the law in ways that advance human capabilities not just in theory but in practice. An example would be to hold polluters accountable for the harm they cause, without placing too heavy a burden on the victims. This would require changes in tort law—in particular, in how causation is established. To mount a legal claim, the tort victim is usually required to specify a harm that has occurred and show causation as well as negligence or intent by the perpetrator. Tort law leaves the burden primarily on the victim, and typically only after harm has already been inflicted; it grants victims preventive measures (a preliminary injunction) only in the case of an imminent and irreversible harm. Moreover, the victim has to be able to identify the perpetrator of harm and often must sue it in a court at its location. These rules make it almost impossible for victims of climate change to hold anyone to account, let alone prevent polluters from inflicting further harm, even when available evidence shows which companies contribute the most to industrial emissions that are accelerating climate change.[41]

From a capabilities perspective, shifting from litigation after harm has been inflicted, and the need to show individual causation, to the precautionary principle would be a major step in the right direction. The precautionary principle states that "if an action or policy has a suspected risk of causing severe harm to the public domain (affecting general health or the environment globally), the action should not be taken in the absence of scientific near-certainty about its safety."[42] Simply stated, if in doubt, don't do it. The precautionary principle reverses the burden of proof and should be applied when there is a high level of probability that the harm will occur, even if substantial uncertainty remains about when and where the harm might materialize.[43]

This is less radical than it might sound. Courts shift the burden of proof in many instances and in the past have come to the aid of consumers by imposing strict liability on companies that produce defective products, for example.[44] Strict liability has also been incorporated into securities law for the misrepresentation of information in prospectuses when a company offers shares to the public. And plaintiffs in securities fraud cases have benefited from a doctrine developed by courts (the "fraud on the market" doctrine) that dispenses plaintiffs of the need to show reliance causation. Instead, courts assume that traders in securities rely on the price signal and, critically, that the price incorporates all relevant information.[45] If courts have the power to incorporate fairly new and unproven theories about the efficiency of financial markets into legal doctrine, they should also be allowed to uphold the precautionary principle in climate-related cases and allow plaintiffs to stop pollution before its full harm has been realized. A JPL could guide courts and thereby also ensure that solutions like these are not perceived as judicial activism with no foundation in the law, but that they are grounded in fundamental principles of justice.

If "do no harm" to bystanders of private action is the minimum requirement for a JPL, "take responsibility" would be the next step. Economic theory holds that efficient outcomes result from the full internalization of the benefits and the costs of using one's assets or resources.[46] Eliminating or reducing the liability of economic actors through law undermines that principle and distorts their incentives for avoiding harm to others. The first culprit is limited liability for shareholders in corporations, which is an off-the-shelf feature of the law of many business organizations. It protects shareholders, including parent companies, from having to take responsibility for the harm "their" corporations cause others. Perhaps this rule was necessary for attracting capital in the early days of industrialization when capital was scarce and the need to broaden the investor base was urgent. Still, California, a successful industrializer, included limited liability in its corporation law only in 1932, which sheds doubt on whether this distortion of responsibility was a necessary prerequisite for industrialization. This legal privilege is certainly misplaced in a world of capital abundance, on the one hand, and existential threats to large parts of humanity that are caused in large part by polluting corporations, on the other.

The U.K. High Court that presided over a case against Royal Dutch Shell said as much when it attributed to the parent company of the multinational group harm that had been caused by its Nigerian subsidiary.[47] The court invoked the duty of care, a fiduciary principle with roots in the law of equity that requires private actors to handle the affairs of others over whom they have control with the requisite care—that is, the care one would apply to one's own affairs. It is the opposite of "moving fast and breaking things," to paraphrase Mark Zuckerberg in describing Facebook's favored business strategy, an approach that is not just tolerated but encouraged by legal shields against liability.[48] If all actors were required by law to take good care of others and treat them with fairness, lest they face liability, much could be accomplished on the path to a more just world that fosters human capabilities. This does not necessarily rule out the use of corporations with separate legal personhood, but would put the burden on shareholders to demonstrate that they are not abusing the corporate form to deflect liability for harm that the corporation imposes on others. Corporate law already has a doctrine to deal with this—piercing the corporate veil—but it is construed excessively narrowly. Only intentional abuse of the form, which also creates grave injustice, will count in many jurisdictions.[49] The revival of the duty-of-care doctrine in cases like *Shell* shows a possible way out of this conundrum.

The principle "take responsibility" could also move contract law in a direction that advances rather than curtails human capabilities. Consent remains the holy grail of binding contracts. Anyone who clicks *agree* is bound to terms that they never read and would not have time to read. The literature has coined the term "dark contracts" to depict consumer contracts that are opaque by design and intended to nudge consumers to sign away many rights or dissuade them from exercising their rights.[50] Tightening the screws even just a little could allow unsuspecting parties to such contracts to challenge them or simply refuse to abide by them. An old doctrine denied parties their day in court if they arrived without "clean hands."[51] A similar principle could be invoked against parties that insist on the notion that contracts are to be honored when the obligations they seek to enforce were imposed and left the other party no room to contest those obligations.

Similar strategies could be employed to deny property-rights claims when the assets in question were acquired by shortchanging the rights of others. Data harvesting occurs regularly without explicit consent and in full denial of legitimate rights that the producers of such data might have, whether those rights are based on property, privacy, or dignity.[52] Courts have consistently denied property-rights protection to personal information, but have readily endorsed the control rights that tech companies have asserted over databases they amassed when consumers did little more than click on the agree button. It is worth recalling that many legal systems deny unsuspecting, bona fide buyers' claims of ownership to goods that were stolen.[53] The same rule could be extended to require data harvesters to show that they rightfully acquired control over data, including that any contracts they used were transparent and fair, not dark.

Companies that use boilerplate contracts will, of course, invoke arbitration clauses to avoid such legal scrutiny by courts. Here too existing legal tools could be invoked to cut through those defenses. Inspiration could come from the so-called breakthrough rule that was used in the EU takeover directive. It requires that domestic corporate law be set aside for the purpose of complying with the directive to ensure that shareholders get to vote on a takeover bid even when a similar right does not exist under domestic law.[54] A similar rule could be used to set aside binding arbitration, choice-of-law, or choice-of-forum clauses to allow weaker parties—consumers or workers—to bring a case to a court that can assess the fairness of the contract in a public forum instead of enforcing formal legal claims behind closed doors, where most arbitration cases are decided.

Much more could, and should, be done to reach a minimum threshold for adequately enabling human capabilities.[55] The suggestions above are just examples of how relatively modest changes, many of which are available in existing law, could improve the law at the margin and set the stage for further change. I am not arguing that transformative change could be achieved by taking these steps, or even that changes to private law alone could usher in a more just law. No doubt, well-crafted housing policies, expanded health care, and an infrastructure that provides clean water and sustainable energy to all would do much to accelerate the pace of change. What I am suggesting is that if we limit ourselves to regulatory law and do not also change private law, including tort and contract law, as well as the procedural rules that govern litigation, little will be achieved, because strategic actors will once again exploit the duality of public and private law to avoid their responsibilities to others.

Further, many social policies are never contemplated or, if adopted, they frequently peter out for lack of funding, an argument that has been weaponized by advocates of balanced budgets or a "black zero."[56] As noted in chapter 1, the monetary system is, next to law, one of the critical social resources that capital has employed for centuries to create wealth for some at the exclusion of others. Money is deeply tied to sovereignty, but in capitalist regimes, money creation has been outsourced to the private sector—to maximize private wealth creation, not social welfare. The Covid crisis demonstrated that states that issue their own currency can lock down large parts of the economy and still provide for their people. It also demonstrated that too many states lack this ability and that, as a result, people living in countries on the periphery of the global monetary system have to endure significantly more hardship.

There is little justification for this state of affairs beyond pointing to history or arguing that money is "inherently" hierarchical.[57] After all, money in all its forms is credit and credit relations can be structured in many different ways. The major difference between private credit and state money is scale. Monetary systems are mutualized systems of credit at scale that involve sovereigns that issue their own money and can backstop it in times of crisis.[58] The state as money issuer promises to accept the money as payment for settlement, and the takers, typically private parties, use it to settle accounts with others as well as with the issuer. The broader the take-up, the stronger the system. Money's inherent hierarchy is directly linked to the capability of maintaining this system without having to depend on others.[59] Whether a sovereign money issuer will make its currency available to others in need—the central banks of other states, domestic and foreign corporations, or households and individuals—is a matter of choice, not something cast in stone. It follows that monetary systems could also be rewired to enhance human capabilities, not just to underwrite private finance.

Instead, in capitalist regimes, the state has "franchised" money creation to private actors—more specifically, to banks—but supports it when the profit motive has driven the system to the brink and the state is required to protect the system from its tendency to self-destruct.[60] The promise to offer state money to backstop private money if and when needed keeps the system afloat, but it is a promise that is made not to the ones in greatest need, and not on the basis of merit, but on the basis of blackmail. Private actors that are big or interdependent enough, such that their downfall would threaten the survival of the system, have a higher chance of survival than others. Bankers and other issuers of private money like this system, of course, because it allows them to reap huge gains while relying on the public to insure them against loss. However, it is not a system that has worked well for democracy, and it certainly has not helped advance the capabilities of people that are pushed to the periphery by its operation.[61] Millions have no access to money, and those who do are often pushed into debt-dependence on private for-profit money issuers.

There is no shortage of alternative visions for a more equitable system of public and private money.[62] Modern technology makes it possible to create a public payment system with everyone linked to a public money issuer, which would cut out the middlemen in the form of private banks.[63] Instead of harnessing the powers of new technology to overhaul the existing system, states are extending the money franchise to issuers of cryptocurrencies. This will likely stabilize these highly volatile currencies but also prolong the life of a monetary system that privatizes gains and socializes costs.

The point bearing emphasis here is that money is a legal matter. Credit conditions, collateral requirements, and margin calls are all legal devices with roots in private law, which has given creditors extensive leverage over debtors. So are the rules that govern central banks and guide their intervention policies. Rescinding the money franchise would be a true game changer for advancing the capabilities approach because it would place the entire system on a more equitable footing. Of course, powerful interests will object to this. The final say over the survival of the current system, however, rests in public hands. It is for legislatures, central banks, or finance ministries to decide whether they wish to create a new banking system in the shadow of the existing one that could spring into action when the next financial crisis looms and they are confronted with another put option: bail us out or else. With an alternative system in place, they could "just say no" without risking a financial meltdown.

A transformative change of private law requires a new normative foundation for private law that is aligned with that of constitutional democracies. This perspective rejects the idea that private law and private actors ever stand outside the boundaries of civility and mutual respect that membership in any community demands. It does not matter whether people contract within domestic legal orders or beyond them, and neither are demands for care and enabling conditions necessarily limited to one's own state or community. Human capabilities are entitlements that all humans have against one another, and especially against entities, public or private, that command power over them or have resources at their disposal that might enable others to realize their capabilities. From a Marxist materialist perspective, this may sound naive. Norms reflect the underlying conditions of production; they are not independent of such conditions and therefore cannot possibly operate as levers of change. If, however, capitalism is understood as a legal regime, as I have argued in this book, this unidirectional way of thinking becomes less persuasive. The law itself is part of the material from which capital is made, and legal institutions facilitate the reconstitution of capitalism. After centuries of capitalism, it is hard to find a sphere that is truly outside, or exogenous to, this process. We therefore must return to the normative foundations of the law to effect a transformative change of capitalism.

Epilogue

Capitalism is a legal regime with features that have allowed it to reconstitute itself, notwithstanding repeated attempts by legislatures to guard against its excesses, often by invoking public law, including regulation. Following Pashukanis, I argue that a critical characteristic of capitalist law is the separation of public and private, each rooted in different normative principles and oftentimes working, not in tandem, but in tension with one another.

Public law is the primary tool available to the state in its interactions with its citizens. Public law is both enabled and constrained by a constitution, by the checks and balances that are built into it, and ultimately by the individual rights that it endorses. Private law, by contrast, empowers private actors to organize their affairs with others under the shadow of the law that affords default rules and offers law enforcement to ensure that commitments are upheld. Capitalist law assumes formal equality of private parties, and although it imposes some restrictions on the abuse of power, it does so only in extreme cases. In many (not all) jurisdictions, only states and their agents and not private actors are bound by constitutional principles; although private actors themselves may invoke such principles against the state, they need not observe these principles in their relations with others. Private power conferred by law is not entirely without limitations. Criminal law establishes red lines, and tort law allows victims of harm to take legal action against an actor that can be shown to have caused the harm. But private law also shields actors from having to take responsibility for conduct that harms even as they profit from such conduct. Limited liability for corporate shareholders is but one example; others include liability ceilings for risky private undertakings, such as operating railroads and nuclear power plants. The costs above that ceiling are socialized, whereas the profits remain in private hands. And although some economic activities that are legally subsidized in this way may be worth the risk from a social perspective, this is not always the case because these activities can result in irreversible damages that future generations will have to bear.

Private law does not only empower private actors to organize their own affairs with one another. It also grants them access to the consolidated means of coercion to enforce their rights against each other, and against the state. The threat of coercive law enforcement adds weight to a claim, but this weight is not distributed equally. It takes resources to litigate. Moreover, not all can use existing access channels to the means of coercion; some may not meet the entry requirements, some may have waived access to court in contracts by consenting to mandatory arbitration clauses, and some may confront a court system that is overburdened and routinely delays justice, especially for small claims. Within the logic of capitalist law, it makes perfect sense for judges to sanction contracts that deny weaker parties access to courts or for state aid to be extended to financial intermediaries in times of crisis, even as it is withheld from people struggling to make ends meet, because capitalism's own survival takes precedence over the fate of mere mortals.[1] However, such a regime can hardly be called just. It does not have to be this way, and experience suggests that stronger labor or consumer-protection laws, or environmental regulation, are feasible under the right political constellations. However, such interventions are always in danger of being unwound, because capitalist law allows powerful private interests to employ private law and individual rights to weaken these legal fixes or erode their efficacy. Global capitalism has vastly increased the options for private actors as conflict-of-law rules have set them loose from their home law to roam the globe and explore other legal pastures.

Conjointly, the three core features of capitalist law—private empowerment, access to the centralized means of coercion, and legal arbitrage—have enabled capitalists (no longer just traders in public debt but traders in any asset that promises financial returns) to create a stranglehold over societies and their quest to govern themselves democratically. Capitalism has survived major crises and, time and again, has been able to get around the guardrails that have been put in place in the aftermath of crises and emerge even stronger.

A possible conclusion from this analysis would be that there is simply no exit from this regime. This conclusion would, however, deny the fact that capitalism is a social, not a natural, system. The economist Douglass North called institutions the "humanly devised constraints that shape human interaction."[2] They may be formal or informal, but they complement and reinforce one another.[3] Institutions are not static but changeable—and not necessarily only along a predetermined path. Transformative institutional change is possible, as history tells us, and it might be accelerated by strategic interventions that set in motion a process that aligns institutions to different norms. As argued in this book, the primacy of private ordering risks undermining the collective order and, moreover, the authority of the law as a social-ordering device. To be accepted as legitimate and induce voluntary compliance with its rule, the law cannot be disjointed from the norms and beliefs that are shared in society. Legitimacy is never guaranteed but must be earned, and as legitimacy wanes, the law loses its authority.

However, like any social construct, the law has the capacity to evolve and to be transformed. Absent this capacity for change, there would not have been a transformation from feudalism to absolutism to republicanism and eventually to democracy, a transformation from colonialism to a new international order, a transformation of post-socialist societies, or indeed, the rise of capitalism. Each of these transformations went hand in hand with legal and institutional change, even if they came with the baggage of old institutions that were not completely overhauled but instead recombined with new ones. Frequently, the changes empowered new actors, such as individuals, cities, or companies, which were able to free themselves from the shackles that came before. "City air makes you free" was a common refrain in Europe when rulers chartered new cities and gave them the power to govern themselves. Freedom was obtained not only from acceding to powerful overlords but also from respecting commoners and undertaking obligations to care for the paupers. Caring has been increasingly relegated to the state, the church, and other charitable organizations, or picked up by members of society that are predisposed or volunteer to do so, often without or for only little pay. Even when care work is paid for, it is underpaid and recognized only in extraordinary times—such as during the Covid pandemic—as essential for societies not only to survive but to thrive. Unfortunately, capitalism has found ways to bring even care into its fold; private equity funds are buying up hospitals and old-age homes and turning them into yet another asset class that can be milked for profits, increasing prices and downgrading the services for those in need.[4]

The question is, When is enough, enough, and when is it time to extend the idea of dignity and self-determination to all, not only to those with resources to claim it? In a world that has come to be dominated by powerful private actors, such a reckoning necessarily requires mechanisms to hold these actors responsible for what they do to others and to constrain their freedom in the name of dignity for all. For this to happen, there must be a normative shift. As long as the logic of capitalism as a freewheeling undertaking of the well-off and powerful prevails, even well-designed new institutions and structures are unlikely to accomplish their goals. And as long as capitalism has the private law to erode restrictions imposed by public law, societies will face an uphill battle in trying to tame capitalism's excesses. Transformative change will require more: a rewiring of the system based on a shift in its normative foundations.

The transformation of the existing system will not happen in a single leap; this is not how history has ever worked. Rather, transformation happens as the cumulative effect of a myriad of smaller steps that form patterns that are mimicked by others in more than one domain of social and economic life or the law. My hope is that this book will make a small contribution toward inspiring such small steps and our ability to recognize these as potential harbingers of transformative change.

Notes

Chapter 1. A Legal Regime

1. Similarly, David Grewal defined it as a juridical system. See David Grewal, "The Legal Constitution of Capitalism," in *After Piketty: The Agenda for Economics and Inequality*, ed. Heather Boushey, J. Bradford DeLong, and Marshall Steinbaum (Cambridge, Mass.: Harvard University Press, 2017), 471–90.

2. See Geoffrey M. Hodgson, *Conceptualizing Capitalism: Institutions, Evolution, Future* (Chicago: University of Chicago Press, 2015). In Hodgson's reading (p. 254), Schumpeter places far greater emphasis on finance than Marx.

3. See John R. Commons, *The Legal Foundations of Capitalism* (New York: Macmillan Company, 1924).

4. On the constitutional foundations of money, see Christine Desan, *Making Money: Coin, Currency, and the Coming of Capitalism* (Oxford: Oxford University Press, 2015). On legal aspects of cryptocurrencies, see Joseph Lee, *Crypto-Finance, Law and Regulation* (Abingdon, U.K.: Routledge, 2022), esp. chap. 5.

5. Katharina Pistor, *The Code of Capital: How the Law Creates Wealth and Inequality* (Princeton, N.J.: Princeton University Press, 2019).

6. Michael Sonenscher, *Capitalism: The Story Behind the Word* (Princeton, N.J.: Princeton University Press, 2022).

7. Sonenscher, *Capitalism*, 37.

8. Sonenscher, *Capitalism*, 64 (highlighting the role of Louis Blanc in particular).

9. Lev Menand, "Lifeblood of the Commonwealth: The Past and Future of Money in America" (unpublished manuscript, 1925) (on file with author).

10. This is more pronounced in some jurisdictions than in others. See the discussion in chapter 3.

11. See, however, the World Bank's assessment regarding the failure of neoliberal policies to bring about prosperity for all. World Bank, *The Challenge of Development* (Oxford: Oxford University Press, 1991).

12. Politicians from Margaret Thatcher to Angela Merkel proclaimed that there is "no alternative" to global capitalism. See Nick Robinson,

"Economy: There Is No Alternative (TINA) Is Back," *BBC News,* March 7, 2013. For a more academic account that defends the system (only) against its abusers, see Raghuram G. Rajan and Luigi Zingales, *Saving Capitalism from the Capitalists: Unleashing the Power of Financial Markets to Create Wealth and Spread Opportunity* (Princeton, N.J.: Princeton University Press, 2004).

13. See, for example, Kristalina Georgieva, "The Economic Possibilities for My Grandchildren" (speech at King's College, Cambridge, U.K., March 14, 2024), https://www.imf.org/en/News/Articles/2024/03/08/sp031424-kings-college-cambridge-kristalina-georgieva.

14. World Bank, *The Challenge of Development;* World Bank, *Economic Growth in the 1990s: Learning from a Decade of Reform* (Washington, D.C.: World Bank, 2005); Dani Rodrik, "Goodbye Washington Consensus, Hello Washington Confusion? A Review of the World Bank's *Economic Growth in the 1990s: Learning from a Decade of Reform,*" *Journal of Economic Literature* 44, no. 4 (2006): 973–87.

15. See Pistor, *The Code of Capital,* chap. 9. Note that Thomas Piketty argues that inequality can be limited by state intervention, in particular its taxing powers. Thomas Piketty, *A Brief History of Equality* (Cambridge, Mass.: Belknap Press of Harvard University Press, 2022). This, however, requires a state that is sufficiently autonomous from the influence of capitalism to take on this task, which has not always been the case.

16. On the management of the great financial crisis, see Adam Tooze, *Crashed: How a Decade of Financial Crises Changed the World* (New York: Viking, 2018). See also Adam Tooze, *Shutdown: How Covid Shook the World's Economy* (New York: Viking, 2021).

17. Stephanie Kelton, *The Deficit Myth: Modern Monetary Theory and the Birth of the People's Economy* (New York: Public Affairs, 2020). The argument holds that the state can always source what it needs and, in principle, faces no hard budget constraints.

18. Jedediah Purdy, *This Land Is Our Land: The Struggle for a New Commonwealth* (Princeton, N.J.: Princeton University Press, 2019). Note, however, that scientists have not sanctioned this designation. See Leigh Philips, "Keep Calm and Carry on with the Anthropocene," *Nation,* March 13, 2024.

19. See Karl Polanyi, *The Great Transformation: The Political and Economic Origins of Our Time* (Boston: Beacon Press, 1944), esp. chap. 7.

20. Mahmood Mamdani, *Citizen and Subject: Contemporary Africa and the Legacy of Late Colonialism* (Princeton, N.J.: Princeton University Press, 1996); Dharma Kumar, *Colonialism, Property and the State* (Delhi: Oxford University Press, 1998); M. B. Hooker, *Legal Pluralism—An Introduction to*

Colonial and Neo-Colonial Laws (Oxford: Clarendon Press, 1975). But for a more benign account of the effects of settler colonialism, see Daron Acemoglu, Simon Johnson, and James Robinson, "Reversal of Fortune: Geography and Institutions in the Making of the Modern World Income Distribution," *Quarterly Journal of Economics* 117, no. 4 (2002), 1231–94.

21. Doreen Lustig, *Veiled Power: International Law and the Private Corporation, 1886–1981* (Oxford: Oxford University Press, 2020); Oscar Gelderblom, "The Organization of Long-Distance Trade in England and the Dutch Republic, 1550–1650," in *The Political Economy of the Dutch Republic*, ed. Oscar Gelderblom (Aldershot, U.K.: Ashgate, 2009), 223–54.

22. Tirthankar Roy and Anand Swamy, *Law and the Economy in Colonial India* (Chicago: University of Chicago Press, 2016).

23. Sally Falk Moore, "Treating Law as Knowledge: Telling Colonial Officers What to Say to Africans About Running Their 'Own' Native Courts," *Law & Society Review* 26, no. 2 (1992): 11–46.

24. See, however, Daron Acemoglu, Simon Johnson, and James A. Robinson, "The Colonial Origins of Comparative Development: An Empirical Investigation," *American Economic Review* 91, no. 5 (2001): 1369–401.

25. Abhishek Chatterjee, "Financial Property Rights Under Colonialism: Some Counterfactual Possibilities," *Journal of Institutional Economics* 12, no. 4 (2016): 797–824.

26. Hooker, *Legal Pluralism*.

27. David Grewal, *Network Power: The Social Dynamics of Globalization* (New Haven, Conn.: Yale University Press, 2008). On money and globalization, see Anush Kapadia, *A Political Theory of Money* (Cambridge: Cambridge University Press, 2024); Stephen J. Choi and Andrew T. Guzman, "National Laws, International Money: Regulation in a Global Capital Market," *Fordham Law Review* 65, no. 5 (1997): 1855–908.

28. David Trubek and Alvaro Santos, *The New Law and Development: A Critical Appraisal* (Cambridge: Cambridge University Press, 2006). See also Katharina Pistor, "The Standardization of Law and Its Effect on Developing Economies," *American Journal of Comparative Law* 50, no. 1 (2002): 101–34.

29. For a critical assessment, see David M. Trubek and Marc Galanter, "Scholars in Self-Estrangement: Some Reflections on the Crisis in Law and Development Studies in the United States," *Wisconsin Law Review* 1974, no. 4 (1974): 1062–102. The prevailing view, however, has changed little. See World Bank, *World Development Report 1996: From Plan to Market* (Washington, D.C.: Oxford University Press, 1996).

30. For details, see the discussion in chapter 2.

31. Andrei Shleifer and Robert W. Vishny, "A Survey of Corporate Governance," *Journal of Finance* 52, no. 2 (1997): 737–83; Rafael La Porta et al., "Law and Finance," *Journal of Political Economy* 106, no. 6 (1998): 1113–55. See also the discussion in chapters 2 and 3.

32. On the importance of precarity, not just inequality, see Albena Azmanova, *Capitalism on Edge: How Fighting Precarity Can Achieve Radical Change Without Crisis or Utopia* (Cambridge: Cambridge University Press, 2020).

33. Ulrich Beck, *Risk Society: Towards a New Modernity* (London: Sage, 1992); Giandomenico Majone, "The Regulatory State and Its Legitimacy Problems," *West European Politics* 22, no. 1 (1999): 1–24; Edward Glaeser and Andrei Shleifer, "The Rise of the Regulatory State," *Journal of Economic Literature* 41, no. 2 (2003): 401–25.

34. Eugene White, "Free Banking During the French Revolution," *Explorations in Economic History* 27 (1990): 151–276; Eugene Nelson White, "The Political Economy of Banking Regulation, 1864–1933," *Journal of Economic History* 42, no. 1 (1982): 33–40; Richard Sylla, John B. Legler, and John J. Wallis, "Banks and State Public Finance in the New Republic: The United States, 1790–1860," *Journal of Economic History* 47, no. 2 (1987): 391–403.

35. Eugene N. White, "Before the Glass-Steagall Act: An Analysis of the Investment Banking Activities of National Banks," *Explorations in Economic History* 23, no. 1 (1986): 33–55; Adam Gordon, "The Creation of Homeownership: How New Deal Changes in Banking Regulation Simultaneously Made Homeownership Accessible to Whites and Out of Reach for Blacks," *Yale Law Journal* 115, no. 1 (2005): 186–226. See also Raghuram G. Rajan and Luigi Zingales, "The Great Reversals: The Politics of Financial Development in the 20th Century," *Journal of Financial Economics* 69, no. 1 (2003): 5–50.

36. Barry Eichengreen, *Globalizing Capital: A History of the International Monetary System,* 2nd ed. (Princeton, N.J.: Princeton University Press, 2008).

37. Carlos Diaz-Alejandro, "Good-Bye Financial Repression, Hello Financial Crash," *Journal of Development Economics* 19, nos. 1–2 (1985): 1–24.

38. Politics played a role in this. See W. G. Gray, "Floating the System: Germany, the United States, and the Breakdown of Bretton Woods, 1969–1973," *Diplomatic History* 31, no. 2 (2007): 295–323. However, private actors using private law were crucial in dismantling capital controls, a key pillar of the system. See Perry Mehrling, *The New Lombard Street: How the Fed Became the Dealer of Last Resort* (Princeton, N.J.: Princeton University Press, 2011).

39. Rawi Abdelal, *Capital Rules* (Cambridge, Mass.: Harvard University Press, 2007).

40. See Mehrling, *The New Lombard Street;* Catherine R. Schenk, "The Origins of the Eurodollar Market in London: 1955–1963," *Explorations in Economic History* 35, no. 2 (1998): 221–38.

41. For a brief overview of the historical context in which this distinction evolved, see Morton J. Horwitz, "The History of the Public/Private Distinction," *University of Pennsylvania Law Review* 130, no. 6 (1982): 1423–28.

42. Morris Cohen and Robert Hale were important scholars in this movement in the United States. See Morris R. Cohen, "Property and Sovereignty," *Cornell Law Quarterly* 13, no. 1 (1927): 8–30; Robert L. Hale, "Coercion and Distribution in a Supposedly Non-Coercive State," *Political Science Quarterly* 38, no. 3 (1923): 470; Robert L. Hale, *Freedom Through Law: Public Control of Private Governing Power* (New York: Columbia University Press, 1952). For a good overview, see also Hanoch Dagan, "Lawmaking for Legal Realists," *Theory and Practice of Legislation* 1, no. 1 (2013): 187–204.

43. This is the position of many legal realists and critical legal studies scholars alike. See Duncan Kennedy, "The States of the Decline of the Public/Private Distinction," *University of Pennsylvania Law Review* 130, no. 6 (1982): 1349–57.

44. Elizabeth Anderson, *Private Government: How Employers Rule Our Lives (and Why We Don't Talk About It)* (Princeton, N.J.: Princeton University Press, 2017), 45 (emphasis added).

45. For a classic account of how a central ruler was able to play off one constituency against another until they finally united against the ruler, see Douglass C. North and Barry R. Weingast, "Constitutions and Commitment: The Evolution of Institutions Governing Public Choice in Seventeenth-Century England," *Journal of Economic History* 49, no. 4 (1989): 803–32.

46. Hanoch Dagan and Avihay Dorfman, *Relational Justice: A Theory of Private Law* (Oxford: Oxford University Press, 2024), 22.

47. Jennifer Graham, "The Rise of Lawfare and Its Implications," *Deseret News,* June 30, 2024.

48. Katharina Pistor and Chenggang Xu, "Incomplete Law," *Journal of International Law and Politics* 35, no. 4 (2003): 931–1013. The role of legislative purpose in guiding courts has always been contested in legal theory because of the need to adapt law to changing circumstances as well. Roscoe Pound, "The Scope and Purpose of Sociological Jurisprudence," *Harvard Law Review* 24, no. 8 (1911): 591–619.

49. Friedrich A. Hayek, *Law, Legislation and Liberty*, vol. 1, *Rules and Order* (Chicago: University of Chicago Press, 1978), 72.

50. On the relation between cultural norms and progressive, formal law, see Gani Aldashev et al., "Formal Law as a Magnet to Reform Custom," *Economic Development and Cultural Change* 6, no. 4 (2012): 795–828. See also Otto Kahn-Freund, "On Uses and Misuses of Comparative Law," *Modern Law Review* 37, no. 1 (1974): 1–27; Lawrence M. Friedman, "Legal Culture and Social Development," *Law & Society Review* 4, no. 1 (1969): 29–44.

51. On modernizing law as an alternative to customs that may be deemed discriminatory by such law, see Aldashev et al., "Formal Law as a Magnet to Reform Custom."

52. For a discussion of these cases, see chapter 3.

53. Christoph Menke, *Critique of Rights* (Cambridge: Polity, 2020). On human rights in particular, see also Samuel Moyn, *Not Enough: Human Rights in an Unequal World* (Cambridge, Mass.: Harvard University Press, 2018).

54. Jamal Greene, *How Rights Went Wrong* (Boston: Houghton Mifflin Harcourt, 2021).

55. The U.S. Supreme Court has narrowed the standing requirements in recent decades. See Spokeo, Inc. v. Robins, 578 U.S. 330 (2016).

56. Anderson, *Private Government*.

57. See chapter 6 for details.

58. Professor Waldron writes that although "the rule of law comprises a requirement that people in positions of authority should exercise their power within a constraining framework of public norms," implicit in the rule of law is "a demand for clearly defined rights of property and contract that can form a basis for stable expectations upheld and enforced by the courts." Jeremy Waldron, "The Rule of Law in Public Law," in *Thoughtfulness and the Rule of Law* (Cambridge, Mass.: Harvard University Press, 2023), 257.

59. Useful summaries of their comments on the state and the law can be found in Hans Kelsen, *The Communist Theory of Law* (London: Stevens & Sons, 1955); Evgeny B. Pashukanis, *Law and Marxism: A General Theory; Towards a Critique of the Fundamental Juridical Concepts* (New York: Routledge Taylor-Francis Group, 2017); Nicos Poulantzas, *State, Power, Socialism*, trans. Patrick Camiller (New York: Verso, 2014).

60. For an excellent overview of these debates within Marxism, see Clyde W. Barrow, "The Marx Problem in Marxian State Theory," *Science & Society* 64, no. 1 (2000): 87–118.

61. John Maynard Keynes, *The General Theory of Employment, Interest and Money* (Orlando, Fla.: Harcourt, 1936); Robert Skidelsky, *Keynes: The Return of the Master* (London: Allen Lane, 2009).

62. Perry Mehrling, "The Vision of Hyman P. Minsky," *Journal of Economic Behavior & Organization* 39, no. 2 (1999): 129–58.

63. Hyman P. Minsky, *Stabilizing an Unstable Economy* (New Haven, Conn.: Yale University Press, 1986).

64. Perry Mehrling, "Minsky and Modern Finance: The Case of Long Term Capital Management," *Journal of Portfolio Management* 26, no. 2 (2000): 81–89.

65. Ricardo Bellofiore, "The Socialization of Investment, from Keynes to Minsky and Beyond," Working Paper No. 822 (Levy Economics Institute of Bard College, December 2014), https://ssrn.com/abstract=2539307.

66. Hale, *Freedom Through Law*.

67. For an excellent summary of this movement and its main contributors, see Samuel Moyn, "Reconstructing Critical Legal Studies," *Yale Law Journal* 134, no. 1 (2024): 77–122.

68. Foundational on the ideas that forged globalization is Quinn Slobodian, *Globalists: The End of Empire and the Birth of Neoliberalism* (Cambridge, Mass.: Harvard University Press, 2018). For a critical review of the different "institutionalisms," see Kathleen Thelen and Sven Steinmo, "Historical Institutionalism in Comparative Politics," in *Structuring Politics: Historical Institutionalism in Comparative Analysis*, ed. Sven Steinmo, Kathleen Thelen, and Frank Longstreth (Cambridge: Cambridge University Press, 1992), 1–32.

69. Max Weber, *Economy and Society: An Outline of Interpretive Sociology*, ed. Guenter Roth and Claus Wittich, trans. Ephraim Fischoff et al., 2 vols. (Berkeley: University of California Press, 1978); John R. Commons, *The Legal Foundations of Capitalism* (New York: Macmillan, 1924); Hale, *Freedom Through Law*; Hodgson, *Conceptualizing Capitalism;* Wolfgang Streeck, *How Will Capitalism End? Essays on a Failing System* (London: Verso, 2016); Wolfgang Streeck, "Taking Capitalism Seriously: Towards an Institutionalist Approach to Contemporary Political Economy," *Socio-Economic Review* 9, no. 1 (2011): 137–67. Note that the label "old" is used to differentiate the institutionalists of the early twentieth century from the new economic institutionalists of the late twentieth century, including Douglass North and Oliver Williamson. See Douglass Cecil North, *Institutions, Institutional Change, and Economic Performance* (Cambridge: Cambridge University Press, 1990); Oliver E. Williamson, *The Economic Institutions of Capitalism: Firms, Markets, Relational Contracting* (New York: Free Press, 1985).

70. Sven Steinmo, "What Is Historical Institutionalism?," in *Approaches in the Social Sciences*, ed. Donatella della Porta and Michael Keating (Cambridge: Cambridge University Press, 2008), 118–38.

71. Simon Deakin et al., "Legal Institutionalism: Capitalism and the Constitutive Role of Law," *Journal of Comparative Economics* 45, no. 1 (2017): 188–200.

72. This in essence is the critique of legal pluralists. See Sally Engle Merry, "Legal Pluralism," *Law & Society Review* 22, no. 5 (1988): 867–96; Brian Z. Tamanaha, "The Folly of the 'Social Scientific' Concept of Legal Pluralism," *Journal of Law and Society* 20, no. 2 (1993): 192–217.

73. For a call to rethink law and the organization of social relations, see Tamara Lothian, *Law and the Wealth of Nations* (New York: Columbia University Press, 2017).

Chapter 2. Theories of Capitalist Law

1. For a representative work, see Poulantzas, *State, Power, Socialism*. The book was first published in 1978, posthumously (in French). For a more recent account, see Jeremy Kessler, "Law and Historical Materialism," *Duke Law Journal* 74 (2025): 1523–95.

2. Olivier Blanchard, Kenneth Froot, and Jeffrey D. Sachs, eds., *The Transition in Eastern Europe*, vol. 2 of 2, *Restructuring*, National Bureau of Economic Research Project Report (Chicago: University of Chicago Press, 1994). For a critique of this approach, see Jon Elster, Claus Offe, and Ulrich K. Preuss, *Institutional Design in Post-Communist Societies: Rebuilding the Ship at Sea* (Cambridge: Cambridge University Press, 1998).

3. On Hungary, see Janos Kornai, "The System Paradigm Revisited," *Revue d'études comparatives Est-Ouest* 48, nos. 1–2 (2017): 239–96.

4. Dalibor Rohac, "Hungary and Poland Aren't Democratic: They're Authoritarian," *Foreign Policy*, February 5, 2018. In 2023, Poland brought the opposition back into power. Monika Scislowska, "Eight Years of Conservative Rule in Poland Ends as Donald Tusk Becomes Prime Minister," *Associated Press*, December 13, 2023. Meanwhile, Viktor Orbán and his Fidesz party have ruled uninterrupted in Hungary since 2010.

5. Polanyi, *The Great Transformation*. Polanyi used this phrase to describe the transformation of society into a market society since the seventeenth century, but also to allude to the possibility of another great transformation after the end of World War II.

6. Jeremy Adelman, "Polanyi, the Failed Prophet of Moral Economics," *Boston Review*, May 30, 2017.

7. Pistor, *The Code of Capital*, 4.

8. Konrad Zweigert and Hein Kötz, *Introduction to Comparative Law* (Oxford: Clarendon Press, 1998); Mary Ann Glendon, Michael Wallace Gordon, and Christopher Osakwe, *Comparative Legal Traditions: Text*,

Material, and Cases on the Civil and Common Law Traditions, with Special Reference to French, German, and English (St. Paul, Minn.: West, 1994).

9. A. G. Chloros, "Common Law, Civil Law, and Socialist Law: Three Leading Systems of the World, Three Kinds of Legal Thought," in *Comparative Legal Cultures,* ed. Csaba Varga (New York: New York University Press, 1992); John Quigley, "The Transformation of Eastern Europe and the Convergence of Socialist and Capitalist Law," *Willamette Law Review* 26, no. 4 (1990): 937–56. See also William E. Butler, *Soviet Law,* 2nd ed. (London: Butterworths, 1988).

10. See Commons, *The Legal Foundations of Capitalism;* Thorstein Veblen, "On the Nature of Capital," *Quarterly Journal of Economics* 22, no. 4 (1908): 517–42.

11. Karl Renner, *The Institutions of Private Law and Their Social Functions,* trans. Eli Ginsberg (New Brunswick, N.J.: Transaction Publishers, 1949). The German original, *Die Rechtsinstitute des Privatrechts und ihre soziale Funktion,* was first published in 1904.

12. Friedrich Engels, *Der Ursprung der Familie, des Privateigentums und des Staates* (Stuttgart: Internationale Bibliothek, 1920).

13. Ironically, a similar point was made more recently regarding the world of corporations by an adherent of a conservative theory of law and economics. See Henry G. Manne, "Our Two Corporation Systems: Law and Economics," *Virginia Law Review* 53, no. 2 (1967): 259–84.

14. Renner, *The Institutions of Private Law and Their Social Functions,* 198.

15. On the latter point, see in particular Avihay Dorfman, "Private Ownership," *Legal Theory* 16, no. 1 (2010): 1–35; Hanoch Dagan, "Inside Property," *University of Toronto Law Journal* 63, no. 1 (2013): 1–21.

16. Renner, *The Institutions of Private Law and Their Social Functions.*

17. Pashukanis, *Law and Marxism,* 56.

18. Pashukanis, *Law and Marxism,* 73.

19. China Mieville, *Between Equal Rights: A Marxist Theory of International Law* (London: Brill Academic Publishing, 2004), esp. chap. 3 ("For Pashukanis: An Exposition and Defense of the Commodity-Form Theory of Law").

20. Mieville, *Between Equal Rights* (building on Chris Arthur's introduction to Pashukanis's theory in Pashukanis, *Law and Marxism*).

21. Pashukanis, *Law and Marxism.* The term "subjective law" refers to the centrality of individual rights in private law in particular. Pashukanis uses the term "subjective law," which stands for the claims that individuals have against others, as opposed to general principles of law that equally affect all.

22. Pashukanis, *Law and Marxism,* 104.

23. Pashukanis, *Law and Marxism*, 144.

24. See Cohen, "Property and Sovereignty"; Hale, *Freedom Through Law*.

25. Pashukanis, *Law and Marxism*, 106.

26. Pashukanis, *Law and Marxism*, 137.

27. A revival is currently underway. See especially Igor Shoikhedbrod, "Private Law's Strange Bedfellows: Why Pashukanis Should Worry Contemporary Formalists," *Canadian Journal of Law & Jurisprudence* 33, no. 2 (2020): 461–79; Rafael Khachaturian, "The State as Social Relation: Poulantzas on Materiality and Political Strategy," in *Research Handbook on Law & Marxism*, ed. Paul O'Connell and Umut Özsu (Northampton, Mass.: Edward Elgar Publishing, 2021), 173–88.

28. Geoffrey Hodgson, *How Economics Forgot History* (London: Routledge, 2001).

29. Peter Hall and David Soskice, *Varieties of Capitalism* (Oxford: Oxford University Press, 2001). See, however, Curtis Milhaupt and Katharina Pistor, *Law and Capitalism: What Corporate Crises Reveal About Legal Systems and Economic Development Around the World* (Chicago: University of Chicago Press, 2008).

30. Poulantzas was born in 1936, a year before Pashukanis was killed, and died by suicide in 1979.

31. Poulantzas, *State, Power, Socialism*, 76.

32. Poulantzas, *State, Power, Socialism*, 76.

33. Poulantzas, *State, Power, Socialism*, 77.

34. Poulantzas, *State, Power, Socialism*, 79. To this one might add that they are equally ignorant of the role that private attorneys, the "masters of the code," play in the production of capital. Pistor, *The Code of Capital*, esp. chap. 7 ("The Masters of the Code").

35. Poulantzas, *State, Power, Socialism*, 69 (emphasis in original).

36. Judith N. Shklar, "The Liberalism of Fear," in *Political Thought and Political Thinkers* (Chicago: University of Chicago Press, 1998), 4–19.

37. Poulantzas, *State, Power, Socialism*, 70.

38. Poulantzas, *State, Power, Socialism*, 73. See also Walter Benjamin, *Toward the Critique of Violence* (Stanford, Calif.: Stanford University Press, 2021); Frank K. Upham, *Law and Social Change in Postwar Japan* (Cambridge, Mass.: Harvard University Press, 1987).

39. Kessler, "Law and Historical Materialism."

40. Indeed, Douglass North received the Nobel Memorial Prize in Economic Sciences for this insight. See Douglass C. North, *Structure and Change in Economic History* (New York: Norton, 1981); North, *Institutions, Institutional Change, and Economic Performance*.

41. La Porta et al., "Law and Finance."

42. Simeon Djankov et al., "The New Comparative Economics," *Journal of Comparative Economics* 31, no. 4 (2003): 595–619.

43. See especially La Porta et al., "Law and Finance."

44. Rafael La Porta et al., "The Quality of Government," *Journal of Law, Economics & Organization* 15, no. 1 (1999): 222–83.

45. Simon Deakin and Katharina Pistor, "Legal Origin Theory: Introduction," in *Legal Origin Theory,* ed. Simon Deakin and Katharina Pistor (Cheltenham, U.K.: Edward Elgar, 2012), viii–xx.

46. On this, see Ross Levine, "Financial Development and Economic Growth: Views and Agenda," *Journal of Economic Literature* 35, no. 2 (1997): 688–726. See also Joseph E. Stiglitz, "Financial Markets and Development," *Oxford Review of Economic Policy* 5, no. 4 (1989): 55.

47. For a different account, see B. L. Anderson, "Law, Finance and Economic Growth in England: Some Long-Term Influences," in *Great Britain and Her World, 1750–1914: Essays in Honour of W. O. Henderson,* ed. Barrie M. Ratcliffe (Manchester, U.K.: Manchester University Press, 1975), 99–124; Naomi R. Lamoreaux and Jean-Laurent Rosenthal, "Legal Regime and Contractual Flexibility: A Comparison of Business's Organizational Choices in France and the United States During the Era of Industrialization," *American Law and Economics Review* 7, no. 1 (2005): 28–61.

48. See Adrian Paukstat, *Staat-Macht-Subjekt: Die Bewegung des Staatsbegriffes bei Michel Foucault und Nicos Poulantzas* (Würzburg: Königshausen & Neumann, 2023), 115, esp. 159 (and accompanying graph).

49. World Bank, *The East Asian Miracle: Economic Growth and Public Policy,* World Bank Policy Research Report (New York: Oxford University Press, 1993). Ignoring its own research results, the World Bank nonetheless endorsed the policies of the Washington Consensus, only to backtrack a decade later. See World Bank, *Economic Growth in the 1990s.*

50. Philip Pettit, *The State* (Princeton, N.J.: Princeton University Press, 2023).

51. Pettit, *The State,* 316.

52. Charles Tilly, "War Making and State Making as Organized Crime," in *Bringing the State Back In,* ed. Peter Evans, Dieter Rueschemeyer, and Theda Skocpol (Cambridge: Cambridge University Press, 1985), 169–91.

53. The same can be said for the analogy he uses to explain his approach. Contrary to views espoused by libertarians, money did not emerge as an invention by merchants who realized how complicated barter is, but was a

product of the state. See Desan, *Making Money;* Roy Kreitner, "Legal History of Money," *Annual Review of Law and Social Science* 8, no. 1 (2012): 415–31.

54. North, *Institutions, Institutional Change, and Economic Performance;* Poulantzas, *State, Power, Socialism,* 173.

55. See especially Max Weber, *General Economic History* (Glencoe, Ill.: Free Press, 1981). This book was published after his death and derived from lecture notes.

56. Alan Scott, "Capitalism, Weber and Democracy," *Max Weber Studies* 1, no. 1 (2000), 45.

57. Poulantzas, *State, Power, Socialism,* 180.

58. Benjamin Braun, "Central Banking and the Infrastructural Power of Finance: The Case of ECB Support for Repo and Securitization Markets," *Socio-Economic Review* 18, no. 2 (2020): 395–418.

59. There has been a profound change in recent years, however, in legal scholarship in the United States and beyond with the rise of law and political economy (LPE) as an alternative to the narrower law and economics approach. Samuel Moyn gives a good overview of the role of LPE as a potential successor to legal realism as well as critical legal studies. See Moyn, "Reconstructing Critical Legal Studies."

60. On efficient contracting from a legal perspective, see Robert E. Scott, "The Law and Economics of Incomplete Contracts," *Annual Review of Law and Social Science* 2 (2006): 279–97. For a similar argument about the market for corporate finance, see Ronald Gilson and Reinier Kraakman, "The Mechanisms of Market Efficiency," *Virginia Law Review* 70, no. 4 (1984): 549–644.

61. Ronald H. Coase, "The Problem of Social Cost," *Journal of Law and Economics* 3 (1960): 1–44. See also Robert C. Ellickson, "Of Coase and Cattle: Dispute Resolution Among Neighbors in Shasta County," *Stanford Law Review* 38, no. 3 (1986): 623–87. Note that Coase himself was more interested in how transaction costs impede the efficient allocation of resources. See the introduction to R. H. Coase, *The Firm, the Market, and the Law* (Chicago: University of Chicago Press, 1990).

62. Louis Kaplow and Stephen Shavell, *Fairness Versus Welfare* (Cambridge, Mass.: Harvard University Press, 2006). But see Piketty, *A Brief History of Equality.*

63. Dorfman, "Private Ownership." See also Hanoch Dagan, *A Liberal Theory of Property* (Cambridge: Cambridge University Press, 2021).

64. Ronald H. Coase, "The Nature of the Firm," *Economica* 4, no. 16 (1937): 386–405.

65. See Oliver Hart and John Moore, "Property Rights and the Nature of the Firm," *Journal of Political Economy* 98, no. 6 (1990): 1119–58.

66. Jonathan Levy, *Ages of American Capitalism* (New York: Random House, 2021).

67. Robin L. West, *Civil Rights: Rethinking Their Natural Foundation* (Cambridge: Cambridge University Press, 2019); Lisa R. Goluboff, "The Thirteenth Amendment and the Lost Origins of Civil Rights," *Duke Law Journal* 50, no. 6 (2001): 1609–86.

68. Connecticut Gen. Life Ins. Co. v. Johnson, 303 U.S. 77, 90 (1938) (Black, J., dissenting).

69. Jedediah Britton-Purdy, Amy Kapczynski, and David Singh Grewal, "Law and Political Economy: Toward a Manifesto," *LPE Blog*, November 6, 2017, https://lpeproject.org/blog/law-and-political-economy-toward-a-manifesto.

70. Moyn, "Reconstructing Critical Legal Studies." See also Roberto Mangabeira Unger, *Law in Modern Society: Toward a Criticism of Social Theory* (New York: Free Press, 1976); Roberto Mangabeira Unger, *What Should Legal Analysis Become?* (New York: Verso, 1996).

71. Moyn, "Reconstructing Critical Legal Studies," 3.

72. Moyn, "Reconstructing Critical Legal Studies," 8.

73. Moyn, "Reconstructing Critical Legal Studies," 23.

74. Kessler, "Law and Historical Materialism."

75. Kessler, "Law and Historical Materialism," 9.

76. G. A. Cohen, *Karl Marx's Theory of History: A Defense* (Princeton, N.J.: Princeton University Press, 1979); Kessler, "Law and Historical Materialism."

77. Poulantzas, *State, Power, Socialism*, 188.

78. Poulantzas, *State, Power, Socialism*, 187 (emphasis in original).

Chapter 3. Legal Empowerment

1. The literature spans different disciplines, most importantly sociology and political science. Renewed attention to political economy has seen a revival of debates about power as well. Key contributors in the field of sociology include Max Weber and Emil Durkheim; in political science, Robert A. Dahl and Robert O. Keohane; in political economy, Karl Marx, Friedrich Engels, Nicos Poulantzas, and Karl Polanyi.

2. See also Robert A. Dahl, *Polyarchy: Participation and Opposition* (New Haven, Conn.: Yale University Press, 1971).

3. I borrow the term "power wielder" from Ruth Grant and Robert O. Keohane, "Accountability and Abuses of Power in World Politics," *American Political Science Review* 99, no. 1 (2005): 29–43.

4. Amir N. Licht, "Social Norms and the Law: Why Peoples Obey the Law," *Review of Law and Economics* 4, no. 3 (2008): 715–50.

5. Pashukanis, *Law and Marxism*.

6. Weber, *Economy and Society*, 2:729–31.

7. J. Stuart Anderson, "Property Rights in Land: Reforming the Heritage," in *The Oxford History of the Laws of England*, vol. 12, *1820–1914 Private Law*, ed. William Cornish et al. (Oxford: Oxford University Press, 2010), 48–78. See also my discussion of these developments in Pistor, *The Code of Capital*, chap. 2.

8. Thomas Piketty, *Capital in the Twenty-First Century*, trans. Arthur Goldhammer (Cambridge, Mass.: Harvard University Press, 2014). See also Pistor, *The Code of Capital*, for a discussion of this "metamorphosis" of capital.

9. David Graeber, *Debt: The First 5,000 Years* (Brooklyn, N.Y.: Melville House, 2011).

10. The attempt by Eric Posner and Glen Weyl to reinvent free markets by subjecting all social relations, including property rights, to the pricing mechanism has revealed that this is a pipe dream. See Eric A. Posner and Glen Weyl, *Radical Markets* (Princeton, N.J.: Princeton University Press, 2018); Hanoch Dagan, "Why Markets? Welfare, Autonomy, and the Just Society," *Michigan Law Review* 117, no. 6 (2019): 1289–311.

11. For a detailed analysis of access to the law-enforcement apparatus, see chapter 5.

12. John Rawls, *A Theory of Justice* (Cambridge, Mass.: Belknap Press of Harvard University Press, 1971), 136–42. See, however, Joel B. Grossman, Herbert M. Kritzer, and Stewart Macaulay, "Do the 'Haves' Still Come Out Ahead?," *Law & Society Review* 33, no. 4 (1999): 803–10.

13. Marc Galanter, "Why the 'Haves' Come Out Ahead: Speculations on the Limits of Legal Change," *Law & Society Review* 9, no. 1 (1974): 95–160.

14. Gary S. Becker, "Crime and Punishment: An Economic Approach," *Journal of Political Economy* 76, no. 2 (1968): 169–217.

15. Dorfman, "Private Ownership." See also Hanoch Dagan and Avihay Dorfman, "The Human Right to Private Property," *Theoretical Inquiries in Law* 18, no. 2 (2017): 391–416. For a comprehensive liberal theory of property law, see Dagan, *A Liberal Theory of Property*.

16. For a brief history, see J. M. Kelly, *A Short History of Western Legal Theory* (Oxford: Clarendon Press, 1992). For a history and critique of the idea of rights from its Greek and Roman roots all the way to Ockham and Hobbes, see Christoph Menke, *Kritik der Rechte* (Berlin: Suhrkamp, 2015).

17. Nadine Strossen, "Recent U.S. and International Judicial Protection of Individual Rights: A Comparative Legal Process Analysis and Proposed Synthesis," *Hastings Law Journal* 41, no. 4 (1990): 805–904.

18. Pistor, *The Code of Capital*, 51–60.

19. Oliver Hart and John Moore, "Property Rights and the Nature of the Firm," *Journal of Political Economy* 98, no. 6 (1990): 1119–58.

20. This was accomplished in the United States by the Computer Fraud and Abuse Act of 1986, Pub. L. No. 99-474, 100 Stat. 1213 (codified at 18 U.S.C. § 1030). In theory, data creators should be able to marshal a property claim to their data by relying on Locke's idea of property through labor. For an extensive discussion and critique of this theory, see Jeremy Waldron, *The Right to Private Property* (Oxford: Oxford University Press, 1988).

21. Noam Schreiber and John Koblin, "Will a Chatbot Write the Next 'Succession'?," *New York Times,* May 2, 2023.

22. Garrett Hardin, "The Tragedy of the Commons," *Science* 1962 (1968): 1243–48. For a critique and extensive evidence on how people actually govern the commons, see Elinor Ostrom, *Governing the Commons—The Evolution of Institutions for Collective Action* (Cambridge: Cambridge University Press, 1990); Elinor Ostrom, "Coping with Tragedies of the Commons," *Annual Review of Political Science* 2, no. 1 (1999): 493–535.

23. Harold Demsetz, "Toward a Theory of Property Rights," *American Economic Review* 57, no. 2 (1967): 347–59.

24. These statutes arguably enabled the "risk society" Beck, *Risk Society.*

25. For a succinct summary, see Richard A. Epstein, "Property Rights and Governance Strategies: How Best to Deal with Land, Water, Intellectual Property, and Spectrum," *Colorado Technology Law Journal* 14, no. 2 (2016): 181–218. For an analysis of how these concepts were appropriated and developed to support European colonization, see Lauren Benton and Benjamin Straumann, "Acquiring Empire by Law: From Roman Doctrine to Early Modern European Practice," *Law and History Review* 28, no. 1 (2010): 1–38. And for an analysis of these concepts in the context of Big Tech's appropriation of data, see Katharina Pistor, "Rule by Data: The End of Markets?," *Law and Contemporary Problems* 83, no. 2 (2020): 101–24.

26. On the importance of abstract rights for the evolution of capitalism, see Weber, *Economy and Society,* vol. 2, chap. 8, sec. 8.

27. Paul Apostolicas, "Silicon States: How Tech Titans Are Acquiring State-Like Powers," *Harvard International Review* 40, no. 4 (2019): 18–21. Seldom discussed, but of increasing importance, is the role of "little tech" in capturing and monetizing consumer data. For an overview of this industry, see Wilneida Negrón, *Little Tech Is Coming for Workers* (Coworker.org, 2021), https://home.coworker.org/wp-content/uploads/2021/11/Little-Tech-Is-Coming-for-Workers.pdf.

28. Stijn Neuteleers, "Trading Nature: When Are Environmental Markets (Un)Desirable?," *Journal of Political Philosophy* 30, no. 1 (2022):

116–39; Robert Watt, "The Fantasy of Carbon Offsetting," *Environmental Politics* 30, no. 7 (2021): 1069–88.

29. Dorfman, "Private Ownership"; Dagan and Dorfman, "The Human Right to Private Property."

30. Ugo Pagano, "The Crisis of Intellectual Monopoly Capitalism," *Cambridge Journal of Economics* 38, no. 6 (2014): 1409–29.

31. See especially Dagan, *A Liberal Theory of Property*.

32. See Dagan, *A Liberal Theory of Property*.

33. Hanoch Dagan, "Pluralism and Perfectionism in Private Law," *Columbia Law Review* 112, no. 6 (2012): 1409.

34. Cedar Point Nursery v. Hassid, 594 U.S. 139 (2018). According to the relevant law, union access was limited to 3 hours per day for 120 days per year. Justice Alito, writing for the majority, declared this to be a "physical invasion" of property (at 140). Justice Breyer, dissenting alongside Justices Sotomayor and Kagan, forcefully disagreed, writing that the law merely "regulated the employers' right to exclude others," as a host of uncontroversial regulations do. For example, he wrote, workplace-safety regulations require corporations to admit inspectors onto the factory floor; wetland-preservation rules require property owners to allow inspection of their coastal lands; elder-protection laws require nursing facilities to do the same. 594 U.S. at 165, 175–76 (Breyer, J., dissenting).

35. Bundesverfassungsgericht [BVerfG] [Federal Constitutional Court], March 1, 1979, BvR 533/77 (Ger.). On the different philosophical roots of property rights in Germany and the United States, see Gregory S. Alexander, "Property as a Fundamental Constitutional Right? The German Example," *Cornell Law Review* 88, no. 3 (2003): 733–78.

36. Basic Law art. 14 (Ger.), available in English at https://www.gesetze-im-internet.de/englisch_gg/englisch_gg.html#p0080.

37. On the role of lawyers as the "masters of the code of capital," see Pistor, *The Code of Capital*, 158–82.

38. For a detailed discussion of case law related to the rights of the Maya, indigenous people residing in what now is the country of Belize, see Pistor, *The Code of Capital*, 23–46.

39. Thomas Merrill and Henry Smith, "Optimal Standardization in the Law of Property: The *Numerus Clausus* Principle," *Yale Law Journal* 110, no. 1 (2000): 1–70.

40. Kean Birch and Fabian Muniesa, *Assetization: Turning Things into Assets in Technoscientific Capitalism* (Cambridge, Mass.: MIT Press, 2020).

41. Ronald Chen and Jon Hanson, "The Illusion of Law: The Legitimating Schemas of Modern Policy and Corporate Law," *Michigan Law Review* 103, no. 1 (2004): 1–149.

42. See *In re* Doubleclick Inc. Privacy Litigation, 154 F. Supp. 2d 497 (S.D.N.Y. 2000) (arguing that individuals do not suffer economic loss when their data are collected). See also Del Vecchio v. Amazon.com, No. C11-366, 2012 WL 1997697, at 4 (W.D. Wash. June 1, 2012) (asserting that plaintiffs' "raw information" is not valuable; it is "just as likely, if not more likely, that Plaintiffs' otherwise non-'economically-exploitable information' gains utility—and thus value—only after it is organized and catalogued by Defendant in a manner that allows advertisers to use it in a targeted fashion").

43. This, in fact, is the position taken by Posner and Weyl, *Radical Markets*.

44. Marietta Auer, *Der privatrechtliche Diskurs der Moderne* (Tübingen, Germany: Mohr Siebeck, 2014) (my translation). The original reads, "Ist ein solches körperliches Eigentum erst einmal anerkannt, drängt es aufgrund des vernunftrechtlichen Mechanismus der Eigentumsbegründung, wonach die individuelle Zwangszuweisung von Eigentumsrechten immer gerechtfertigt ist, wenn knappe Güter nur durch individuelle Arbeit bzw. Okkupation entstehen oder nutzbar gemacht werden können, von selbst in die Richtung immer weitergehender Propertisierung der individuellen Persönlichkeitssphäre."

45. The Coase theorem was derived from Coase's article on the problem of social costs. Coase, "The Problem of Social Cost." As Coase himself noted, he did not coin the term "Coase theorem"; George Stigler did. Neither did he mean to place the ideal world of an economy with no transaction costs at the center of economists' attention, which he invariably did, and which helped him secure the Nobel Memorial Prize in Economic Sciences. His original intention was to focus on the problem of social costs. See his introduction to Coase, *The Firm, the Market, and the Law*.

46. Robert Scott, "The Law and Economics of Incomplete Contracts," *Annual Review of Law and Social Science* 2 (2006): 279–97.

47. The legal rules on who bears the costs of litigation vary by jurisdiction. In some jurisdictions, the loser pays all costs in the end, whereas in others, each party has to pay its own lawyers no matter the outcome. See Peter Karsten and Oliver Bateman, "Detecting Good Public Policy Rationales for the American Rule: A Response to the Ill-Conceived Calls for 'Loser Pays' Rules," *Duke Law Journal* 66, no. 3 (2016): 729–61.

48. Frank Upham, *The Great Property Fallacy: Theory, Reality, and Growth in Developing Countries* (Cambridge: Cambridge University Press, 2018), 45–51.

49. Upham, *The Great Property Fallacy*, 46.

50. Upham, *The Great Property Fallacy*, 48.

51. Craig Rotherham, "Property and Power: The Judicial Redistribution of Proprietary Rights," in *Private Law and Power*, ed. Kit Barker et al. (Oxford: Hart Publishing, 2017), 107–36.

52. Cass Sunstein has suggested that this type of judicial power belonged to an early stage in the history of American law and has since been replaced by the rise of the administrative state. Cass Sunstein, "Interpreting Statutes in the Regulatory State," *Harvard Law Review* 103, no. 2 (1989): 405–508. However, this has arguably been reversed by the activism of the Roberts court.

53. Cited in Rotherham, "Property and Power," 114.

54. Rotherham, "Property and Power," 112.

55. Guido Calabresi and Douglas Melamed, "Property Rules, Liability Rules, and Inalienability: One View of the Cathedral," *Harvard Law Review* 85, no. 6 (1972): 1090.

56. This bears resemblance to the classification of property rules under Roman law, which, as discussed in chapter 1, distinguished between assets that were already appropriated, assets that were appropriable, and assets that were held in common.

57. Calabresi and Melamed, "Property Rules, Liability Rules, and Inalienability." The next generation of law and economics scholars has argued to the contrary that social welfare is best achieved by individual choice and individual transactions, not by insisting on morals and norms. See Kaplow and Shavell, *Fairness Versus Welfare*.

58. "Shell to Pay 15 Mln Euros to Nigerian Farmers over Pollution," *Barron's*, December 23, 2022.

59. Okpabi v. Royal Dutch Shell Plc, [2021] UKSC 3.

60. Sea-Land Services Inc. v. Pepper Source, 993 F.2d 1309 (7th Cir. 1993). Empirical studies have shown that claims seeking to pierce the corporate veil rarely succeed. See Robert Thompson, "Piercing the Corporate Veil: An Empirical Study," *Cornell Law Review* 76, no. 5 (1991): 1036–74.

61. Terra Lawson-Remer, "Property Insecurity," *Brooklyn Journal of International Law* 38, no. 1 (2012): 145–91.

62. Acemoglu, Johnson, and Robinson, "The Colonial Origins of Comparative Development."

63. For a discussion and critical assessment of property rights and other indicators that have been widely used in them, see Katharina Pistor, "Re-Construction of Private Indicators for Public Purpose," in *Governance by Indicators: Global Power Through Quantification and Rankings*, ed. Kevin Davis, Benedict Kingsbury, and Sally Engle Merry (Oxford: Oxford University Press, 2012), 165–79.

64. Abhijit Banerjee and Lakshmi Iyer, "History, Institutions, and Economic Performance: The Legacy of Colonial Land Tenure Systems in India," *American Economic Review* 95, no. 4 (2005): 1190–213.

65. For details, see Upham, *The Great Property Fallacy*, 62–81.

66. Madhav Khosla, *India's Founding Moment: The Constitution of a Most Surprising Democracy* (Cambridge, Mass.: Harvard University Press, 2020).

67. Rachel E. Kranton and Anand V. Swamy, "The Hazards of Piecemeal Reform: British Civil Courts and the Credit Market in Colonial India," *Journal of Development Economics* 58 (1999): 1–24; Tirthankar Roy and Anand V. Swamy, *Law and the Economy in Colonial India* (Chicago: University of Chicago Press, 2016). On the long-term effects of this colonial policy, see also Banerjee and Iyer, "History, Institutions, and Economic Performance."

68. Rashmi Venkatesan, "The Evolution of the Right to Property in India: From a Law and Development Perspective," *Law and Development Review* 14, no. 1 (2021): 279–81.

69. Venkatesan, "The Evolution of the Right to Property in India," 275.

70. Ruth Hall and Thembela Kepe, "Elite Capture and State Neglect: New Evidence on South Africa's Land Reform," *Review of African Political Economy* 44, no. 151 (2017): 122–30; Roy Jankielsohn and André Duvenhage, "Expectations and the Issue of Land in South Africa—the Historical Origins and Current Debate," *New Contree* 80, no 1 (2018): 22–47.

71. Edward Lahiff, "From 'Willing Seller, Willing Buyer' to a People-Driven Land Reform," Policy Brief No. 17 (Institute for Poverty, Land, and Agrarian Studies, 2005).

72. Expropriation Law, chap. 5, art. 12(3) (S. Afr.).

73. Marianna Merten, "Controversial Expropriation Bill Is Finally Approved After Navigating a 14-Year Rocky Road," *Daily Maverick* (South Africa), September 29, 2022.

74. Michael Heller, *Gridlock Economics: How Too Much Ownership Wrecks Markets, Stops Innovation, and Costs Lives* (New York: Basic Books, 2008); Michael Heller, "The Tragedy of the Anti-Commons: Property in the Transition from Marx to Markets," *Harvard Law Review* 111, no. 3 (1998): 621–88.

75. ESG is a relatively new acronym that has replaced "corporate social responsibility" and was widely embraced by investors and companies before the political backlash that occurred, especially in the southern United States. See Stefan J. Padfield, "An Introduction to Anti-ESG Legislation," *Transactions: The Tennessee Journal of Business and Law* 24, no. 2 (2023): 291–329.

76. The countries that have withdrawn include Spain, France, the Netherlands, and Germany, among other EU nations. Monika Dulian, European Parliamentary Research Service, PE 754.632, "EU Withdrawal from the Energy Charter Treaty" (December 2023), https://www.europarl.europa.eu/RegData/etudes/BRIE/2023/754632/EPRS_BRI(2023)754632_EN.pdf. On how difficult it is to get out from under international investor-protection treaties, see Federico M. Lavopa, Lucas E. Barreiros, and Victoria M. Bruno, "How to Kill a BIT and Not Die Trying: Legal and Political Challenges of Denouncing or Renegotiating Bilateral Investment Treaties," *Journal of International Economic Law* 16, no. 4 (2013): 869–91.

77. Elizabeth Fortin, "Reforming Land Rights: The World Bank and the Globalization of Agriculture," *Social and Legal Studies* 14, no. 2 (2005): 147–77.

78. William Blackstone, *Commentaries on the Laws of England*, vol. 1 (1765; facsimile ed., Chicago: University of Chicago Press, 1979).

79. Julie Cohen uses the term "informational capitalism" to describe the current age. See Julie E. Cohen, *Between Truth and Power: The Legal Construction of Informational Capitalism* (Oxford: Oxford University Press, 2019). By contrast, Shoshana Zuboff prefers the term "surveillance capitalism." See Shoshana Zuboff, *The Age of Surveillance Capitalism: The Fight for a Human Future at the New Frontier of Power* (New York: PublicAffairs, 2019).

80. On the extraterritorial reach of EU regulation, see Anu Bradford, *The Brussels Effect: How the European Union Rules the World* (Oxford: Oxford University Press, 2020).

81. Statistics are for 2024 from DataReportal, *Digital 2024: Global Overview Report* (2024), https://datareportal.com/reports/digital-2024-global-overview-report.

82. Grewal, *Network Power*.

83. Paul Weiler, "Promises to Keep: Securing Workers' Rights to Self-Organization Under the NLRA," *Harvard Law Review* 96, no. 8 (1983): 1769–827.

84. Data available from the OECD portal.

85. See Duplex Printing Press Co. v. Deering, 254 U.S. 443 (1921).

86. See the discussion of the *Cedar Point Nursery* case in note 34.

87. Melissa Eddy, "Tesla Strike Is a Culture Clash: Swedish Labor vs. American Management," *New York Times*, November 27, 2023. Musk's anti-union business practices are part of his public persona. In August 2024, the United Automobile Workers (UAW) filed federal unfair-labor-practice charges against Musk and Donald Trump after Trump praised Musk for firing striking workers in a live conversation streamed on X, the social-media

platform owned by Musk. See Tim Balk, "UAW Files Labor Charges Against Trump and Musk Over Interview," *New York Times*, August 13, 2024.

88. Guillaume Amouret, "'I'll Stay on Strike for Months or Even Years to Get This Collective Agreement': In Sweden, the Fight Against Tesla Continues," *Equal Times*, July 1, 2024.

89. Umar Shakir, "Tesla Sues Sweden's Postal Agency and Wins as Union Fight Escalates," *The Verge*, November 27, 2023.

90. Peter A. Hall and David Soskice, *Varieties of Capitalism* (Oxford: Oxford University Press, 2001); Alan Siaroff, "Corporatism in 24 Industrial Democracies: Meaning and Measurement," *European Journal of Policy Research* 36, no. 2 (1999): 175–205.

91. Lucian Bebchuk and Mark Roe, "A Theory of Path Dependence in Corporate Ownership and Governance," *Stanford Law Review* 52, no. 1 (1999): 127–70.

92. See Galanter, "Why the 'Haves' Come Out Ahead."

93. John H. Dunning and Rajneesh Narula, eds., *Foreign Direct Investment and Governments: Catalysts for Economic Restructuring* (New York: Routledge, 1995).

94. Eswar Prasad, Raghuram Rajan, and Arvind Subramanian, "Foreign Capital and Economic Growth," *Brookings Papers on Economic Activity* 2007, no. 1 (2007): 153–231. Asli Leblebicioğlu and Jessica Madariaga, "Financial Flows, Composition of Capital, and Growth," *IMF Economic Review* 63, no. 2 (2015): 325–52.

95. William Olney, "A Race to the Bottom? Employment Protection and Foreign Direct Investment," *Journal of International Economics* 91, no. 2 (2013): 191–203.

96. Article 3 of the original treaty establishes the obligation of member states to eliminate restrictions on the free movement of goods, people, services, and capital.

97. In the European Union, the Court of Justice of the European Union is still upholding nondiscrimination principles to protect temp workers from more egregious practices, such as a refusal to give them an explanation for being fired. See Case C-715/20, K.L v. X sp. z o.o (ECLI:EU:C:2024:139), a case referred by a Polish court, decided on February 20, 2024.

98. See "Temporary Employment," OECD, https://www.oecd.org/en/data/indicators/temporary-employment.html.

99. See also chapter 5 on legal arbitrage.

100. Mary L. Gray and Siddharth Suri, *Ghost Work* (Boston: Houghton Mifflin Harcourt, 2019).

101. This is how Amazon advertises its platform. See Amazon Mechanical Turk, https://www.mturk.com.

Chapter 4. Access to Legal Coercion

1. See Robert H. Bates, *Prosperity and Violence: The Political Economy of Development* (New York: W. W. Norton, 2001).

2. Douglass C. North, John Joseph Wallis, and Barry R. Weingast, *Violence and Social Orders: A Conceptual Framework for Interpreting Recorded Human History* (Cambridge: Cambridge University Press, 2009).

3. Weber, *Economy and Society;* Geoffrey M. Hodgson, "On the Institutional Foundations of Law: The Insufficiency of Custom and Private Ordering," *Journal of Economic Issues* 43, no. 1 (2009): 143–66; Timothy Besley and Torsten Persson, "State Capacity, Conflict, and Development," *Econometrica* 78, no. 1 (2010): 1–34.

4. North and Weingast, "Constitutions and Commitment."

5. Hodgson, in "On the Institutional Foundations of Law," makes the important point that the law suppresses customs in the name of stability.

6. Alexander Stille, *Excellent Cadavers: The Mafia and the Death of the First Italian Republic* (New York: Pantheon Books, 1995); Diego Gambetta, *The Sicilian Mafia* (Cambridge, Mass.: Harvard University Press, 1993). See also Curtis J. Milhaupt and Mark D. West, "The Dark Side of Private Ordering: An Institutional and Empirical Analysis of Organized Crime," *University of Chicago Law Review* 67, no. 1 (2000): 41–95.

7. On the term "failed states" and its use, see Olivier Nay, "Fragile Failed States: Critical Perspectives on Conceptual Hybrids," *International Political Science Review* 34, no. 3 (2013): 326–41.

8. Charles Tilly, "War Making and State Making as Organized Crime."

9. Charles Howard McIlwain, *Constitutionalism: Ancient and Modern* (Ithaca, N.Y.: Cornell University Press, 1947); Stephen Holmes, "Constitutionalism," in *The Encyclopedia of Democracy,* ed. Seymour Martin Lipset, vol. 1 (London: Routledge, 1995), 299–305.

10. Thomas Hobbes, *Hobbes's Leviathan* (1651; repr., Oxford: Oxford University Press, 1947).

11. The ideas that inform these mechanisms have a long history. Many were formed during the Enlightenment and refined over the development of modern Western democracies, especially as the colonial era gave way to globalized economies. See Robert O. Keohane, "Hobbes's Dilemma and Institutional Change in World Politics: Sovereignty in International Society," in *Whose World Order? Uneven Globalization and the End of the Cold War,* ed. Hans-Henrik Holm and Georg Sørensen (New York: Routledge, 1995), 165–86.

12. Claire Priest, "Enforcing Sympathy: Animal Cruelty Doctrine After the Civil War," *Law & Social Inquiry* 44, no. 1 (2019): 136–69.

13. Priest, "Enforcing Sympathy," 140–41.

14. Rebecca M. Ryan, "The Sex Right: A Legal History of the Marital Rape Exemption," *Law & Social Inquiry* 20, no. 4 (1995): 941–1001.

15. Andrew Fede, "Legitimized Violent Slave Abuse in the American South, 1619–1865: A Case Study of Law and Social Change in Six Southern States," *American Journal of Legal History* 29, no. 2 (1985): 93–150.

16. Albert Breton et al., eds., *Multijuralism: Manifestations, Causes, and Consequences* (Williston, Vt.: Ashgate, 2009).

17. Katharina Pistor, Antara Haldar, and Amrit Amirapu, "Social Norms, Rule of Law, and Gender Reality: An Essay on the Limits of the Dominant Rule of Law Paradigm," in *Global Perspectives on the Rule of Law*, ed. James Heckman, Robert L. Nelson, and Lee Cabatingan (London: Routledge-Cavendish, 2010), 241–78.

18. Anderson, *Private Government*.

19. See Fibreboard v. NLRB, 403 U.S. 905 (1973).

20. Katharina Pistor, "Codetermination: A Sociopolitical Model with Governance Externalities," in *Employees and Corporate Governance*, ed. Margaret M. Blair and J. Mark Roe (Washington, D.C.: Brookings Institution Press, 1999), 163–93; Gary Gorton and Frank A. Schmid, "Capital, Labor, and the Firm: A Study of German Codetermination," *Journal of the European Economic Association* 2, no. 5 (2004): 863–905.

21. Lynn A. Stout, "Derivatives and the Legal Origin of the 2008 Credit Crisis," *Harvard Business Law Review* 1, no. 1 (2011): 1–38. See also Edward R. Morrison, Mark J. Roe, and Christopher S. Sontchi, "Rolling Back the Repo Safe Harbors," *Business Lawyer* 69, no. 4 (2014): 1016–47, who critique the preferential treatment of derivatives in bankruptcy.

22. The principle goes back to Roman law and is widely held to be foundational for modern legal systems. And yet for many victims of harm it remains under-enforced, as courts often fail to hold anybody liable for damage that has been inflicted. See Abimbola A. Olowofoyeku, "When Courts Get It Wrong: Judicial Errors and Common Law Underenforcement," *Law Quarterly Review* 134 (2018): 450–77.

23. *In re* Doubleclick Inc. Privacy Litigation, 154 F. Supp. 2d 497 (S.D.N.Y. 2000).

24. *In re* iPhone Application Litigation, 844 F. Supp. 2d 1040, 1063 (N.D. Cal. 2012).

25. The text of the provision is available at Legal Information Institute, https://www.law.cornell.edu/constitution/articleiii.

26. Spokeo, Inc. v. Robins, 578 U.S. 330, 340 (2016).

27. Fair Credit Reporting Act of 1970 (FCRA), 15 U.S.C. §§ 1681–1681x.

28. See *Spokeo*, 578 U.S. at 350 (Ginsburg, J., dissenting).

29. Ernest Metzger, "Action," in *A Companion to Justinian's Institutes*, ed. Ernest Metzger (London: Duckworth, 1998), 208–28.

30. Metzger, "Action."

31. Women's Business Ownership Act of 1988, Pub. L. No. 100-533, 102 Stat. 2689; chapter 200 of the Laws of New York, 1848.

32. Kelly M. Kennington, *In the Shadow of Dred Scott: St. Louis Freedom Suits and the Legal Culture of Slavery in Antebellum America* (Athens: University of Georgia Press, 2017), 2–3.

33. Katherine Franke, *Repair: Slavery's Unfinished Business* (Chicago: Haymarket Books, 2019).

34. For the United Kingdom, see the 1837 Slave Compensation Act, 1 & 2 Vict c.3. For the United States, see Kris Manjapra, "DC's Enslavers Got Reparations: Freed People Got Nothing," *Politico*, June 17, 2022. Moreover, empirical research has shown that former slave owners quickly made up for their economic losses, whereas freed Black people never did. See Philipp Ager, Leah Boustan, and Katherine Eriksson, "The Intergenerational Effects of a Large Wealth Shock: White Southerners After the Civil War," *American Economic Review* 111, no. 11 (2021): 3767–94.

35. Brittany Farr, "Breach by Violence: The Forgotten History of Sharecropper Litigation in the Post-Slavery South," *UCLA Law Review* 69, no. 3 (2022): 674–745.

36. Robin L. West, *Civil Rights: Rethinking Their Natural Foundation* (Cambridge: Cambridge University Press, 2019).

37. Cheryl I. Harris, "Whiteness as Property," *Harvard Law Review* 106, no. 8 (1993): 1707–91.

38. See section 307 of the Revised Uniform Partnership Act of 1997; Federal Rules of Civil Procedure 17(b)(3)(A). ("Capacity to sue or be sued is determined . . . by the law of the state where the court is located, except that . . . a partnership or other unincorporated association with no such capacity under that state's law may sue or be sued in its common name to enforce a substantive right existing under the United States Constitution or laws . . . .")

39. On how labor unions have been restricted in their ability to organize labor in the United States, see chapter 3.

40. For an overview of the debate about the rights of nature, see Tiffany Challe, "The Rights of Nature—Can an Ecosystem Bear Legal Rights?," *State of the Planet* (Columbia Climate School), https://news.climate.columbia.edu/2021/04/22/rights-of-nature-lawsuits.

41. Paul D. Carrington, "Protecting the Right of Citizens to Aggregate Small Claims Against Businesses," *University of Michigan Journal of Law*

Reform 46, no. 2 (2013): 537–48. Whether this is the only or best strategy for protecting the legally weak is an open question. Many continental European countries rely to a greater extent on consumer-protection laws that enhance the contractual rights of consumers or regulate the contracts directly.

42. On the 1966 reforms and the shift from "opt into" to automatic inclusion, see Brian T. Fitzpatrick, "The Ironic History of Class Actions," in *The Conservative Case for Class Actions* (Chicago: University of Chicago Press, 2019), 7–17.

43. Myriam Gilles and Gary Friedman, "Exploding the Class Action Agency Costs Myth: The Social Utility of Entrepreneurial Lawyers," *University of Pennsylvania Law Review* 155, no. 1 (2006): 103–04.

44. Linda A. Mullenix, "Ending Class Actions as We Know Them: Rethinking the American Class Action," *Emory Law Journal* 64, no. 2 (2014): 399–449 (quote at 410).

45. John Fabian Witt, *The Accidental Republic: Crippled Workingmen, Destitute Widows, and the Remaking of American Law* (Cambridge, Mass.: Harvard University Press, 2006).

46. Christine P. Bartholomew, "Redefining Prey and Predator in Class Actions," *Brooklyn Law Review* 80, no. 3 (2015): 743–806.

47. Carrington, "Protecting the Right of Citizens to Aggregate Small Claims Against Businesses."

48. Strike suits are often brought without actual evidence of wrongdoing, but merely because of a significant change in share prices or other indicators that do not necessarily indicate wrongdoing.

49. The relevant legislative reforms are the Private Securities Litigation Reform Act of 1995 (PSLRA) and the Securities Litigation Uniform Standards Act of 1998 (SLUSA).

50. For an assessment of the quality of legislative intervention, see Joseph A. Grundfest and A. C. Pritchard, "Statutes with Multiple Personality Disorders: The Value of Ambiguity in Statutory Design and Interpretation," *Stanford Law Review* 54, no. 4 (2002): 627–736. See also Stephen B. Burbank, "The Class Action Fairness Act of 2005 in Historical Context: A Preliminary View," *University of Pennsylvania Law Review* 156, no. 6 (2008): 1439–551.

51. Ralf Michaels, "Der Code des Kapitals und seiner Portabilität," *RabelsZ* 85, no. 4 (2021): 890–906; Ralf Michaels and Nils Jansen, "Private Law Beyond the State? Europeanization, Globalization, Privatization," *American Journal of Comparative Law* 54, no. 4 (2006): 843–90.

52. Many fast-food chains, including McDonald's, are franchises.

53. Robert Hockett and Saule T. Omarova, "The Finance Franchise," *Cornell Law Review* 102, no. 5 (2017): 1143–218.

54. Article V of the United Nations Convention on the Recognition and Enforcement of Foreign Arbitral Awards ("New York Convention"), available at https://www.newyorkconvention.org/english. See also article 34 of the UNCITRAL Model Law on International Commercial Arbitration, available at https://uncitral.un.org/en/texts/arbitration/modellaw/commercial_arbitration.

55. Convention of 2 July 2019 on the Recognition and Enforcement of Foreign Judgments in Civil or Commercial Matters, available at https://www.hcch.net/en/instruments/conventions/full-text/?cid=137.

56. Pilar Domingo, "Judicial Independence and Judicial Reform in Latin America," in *The Self-Restraining State: Power and Accountability of New Democracies,* ed. Andreas Schedler, Larry Diamond, and Marc F. Plattner (Boulder: Lynne Rienner Publishers, 1999), 151–76; Sergio Bartole, "Alternative Models of Judicial Independence: Organizing the Judiciary in Central and Eastern Europe," *East European Constitutional Review,* Winter 1998, 62–69; Jennifer Widner, "Building Judicial Independence in Common Law Africa," in Schedler et al., *The Self-Restraining State,* 177–93.

57. Maria L. Marcus, "Judicial Overload: The Reasons and the Remedies," *Buffalo Law Review* 28, no. 1 (1979): 111–41.

58. Myriam Gilles, "Class Warfare: The Disappearance of Low-Income Litigants from the Civil Docket," *Emory Law Journal* 65, no. 6 (2016): 1531–68. For U.S. state courts, see also Anna E. Carpenter et al., "Judges in Lawyerless Courts," *Georgetown Law Journal* 110, no. 3 (2022): 509–67.

59. Judith Resnik, "Diffusing Disputes: The Public in the Private of Arbitration, the Private in Courts, and the Erasure of Rights," *Yale Law Journal* 124, no. 8 (2015): 2804–939.

60. AT&T Mobility LLC v. Concepcion, 131 S. Ct. 1740 (2011).

61. David S. Clancy and Matthew M. K. Stein, "An Uninvited Guest: Class Arbitration and the Federal Arbitration Act's Legislative History," *Business Lawyer* 63, no. 1 (2007): 58.

62. For a critical assessment of Justice Scalia's assertion, see Deepak Gupta and Lina Khan, "Arbitration as Wealth Transfer," *Yale Law & Policy Review* 25 (2017): 499–520.

63. DirectTV, Inc. v Imburgia, 577 U.S. 47 (2015) (consumer contracts); Epic Systems Corp. v. Lewis, 138 S. Ct. 1612 (2018) (employment).

64. Consumer Financial Protection Bureau, *Arbitration Study: Report to Congress, Pursuant to Dodd-Frank Wall Street Reform and Consumer Protection Act §1028(a)* (2015), 8 (table 1).

65. Consumer Financial Protection Bureau, *Arbitration Study.*

66. Directive 2013/11/EU of the European Parliament and of the Council of 21 May 2013 on Alternative Dispute Resolution for Consumer

Disputes and Amending Regulation (EC) No 2006/2004 and Directive 2009/22/EC (Directive on Consumer ADR), available at https://eur-lex.europa.eu/eli/dir/2013/11/oj.

67. Stefaan Voet et al., "Recommendations from Academic Research Regarding Future Needs of the EU Framework of the Consumer Alternative Dispute Resolution (ADR)," Report JUST/2020/CONS/FW/CO03/0196 (KU Leuven, June 2022).

68. Quoted in Gupta and Khan, "Arbitration as Wealth Transfer," 499.

69. Avner Greif, *Institutions and the Path to the Modern Economy: Lessons from Medieval Trade* (Cambridge: Cambridge University Press, 2006).

70. Anthony T. Kronman, "Contract Law and the State of Nature," *Journal of Law, Economics & Organization* 1, no. 1 (1985): 5–32.

71. For details, see Kronman, "Contract Law and the State of Nature."

72. Laurie S. Goodman and Christopher Mayer, "Homeownership and the American Dream," *Journal of Economic Perspectives* 32, no. 1 (2018): 31–58.

73. See Kronman, "Contract Law and the State of Nature."

74. Nakita Cuttino, "The Rise of 'FringeTech': Regulatory Risks in Earned-Wage Access," *Northwestern University Law Review* 115, no. 6 (2021): 1505–79.

75. Primavera De Filippi and Aaron Wright, *Blockchain and the Law* (Cambridge, Mass.: Harvard University Press, 2018).

76. Kevin Werbach and Nicolas Cornell, "Contracts *Ex Machina*," *Duke Law Journal* 67, no. 2 (2017): 313–82 (quote at 367).

77. See chapter 3 for a discussion of disembedded purpose contracts (Max Weber).

78. On the importance of the legal *form* as opposed to the contents or substance of the law, see the discussion of Pashukanis's arguments in chapter 2.

Chapter 5. Legal Arbitrage

1. William Sharpe and Gordon Alexander, *Investments*, 4th ed. (Englewood Cliffs, N.J.: Prentice Hall, 1990), 283.

2. Victor Fleischer, "Regulatory Arbitrage," *Texas Law Review* 89, no. 2 (2010): 227–90.

3. Jan Friedrich and Matthias Thiemann, "The Economic, Legal and Social Dimension of Regulatory Arbitrage," *Accounting, Economics, and Law* 11, no. 2 (2021): 81–90 (quote at 81).

4. Katharina Pistor and Chenggang Xu, "Incomplete Law," *Journal of International Law and Politics* 35, no. 4 (2003): 931–1013.

5. Joseph A. Grundfest and A. C. Pritchard, "Statutes with Multiple Personality Disorders: The Value of Ambiguity in Statutory Design and Interpretation," *Stanford Law Review* 54, no. 4 (2002): 627–736.

6. Oliver Hart and John Moore, "Foundations of Incomplete Contracts," *Review of Economic Studies* 66, no. 1 (1999): 115–38; Eric Maskin and Jean A. F. Tirole, "Unforeseen Contingencies and Incomplete Contracts," *Review of Economic Studies* 66, no. 1 (1999): 83–114.

7. Victor Goldberg, "Regulation and Administered Contracts," *Bell Journal of Economics* 7, no. 2 (1976): 426–52; Pistor and Xu, "Incomplete Law."

8. Louis Kaplow, "Rules Versus Standards: An Economic Analysis," *Duke Law Journal* 42, no 3 (1992): 557–629.

9. Michael Love, "Who Benefits from Partnership Flexibility?" (unpublished manuscript, October 2024) (on file with author).

10. Thomas Piketty, *Capital and Ideology*, trans. Arthur Goldhammer (Cambridge, Mass.: Belknap Press of Harvard University Press, 2020).

11. Wolfgang Streeck and Kathleen Thelen, "Introduction: Institutional Change in Advanced Political Economies," in *Beyond Continuity: Institutional Change in Advanced Political Economies*, ed. Wolfgang Streeck and Kathleen Thelen (Oxford: Oxford University Press, 2005), 1–39.

12. "Minimum Wage," U.S. Department of Labor, https://www.dol.gov/general/topic/wages/minimumwage.

13. See the various cases studies in Pistor, *The Code of Capital*.

14. For financial laws and regulations in particular, see Matthias Thiemann, *Out of the Shadows?* (Cambridge: Cambridge University Press, 2020).

15. Article 5(3) of the Treaty on European Union, available at http://data.europa.eu/eli/treaty/teu_2016/oj.

16. The extraterritorial reach of U.S. securities law was curtailed by the Supreme Court in Morrison v. National Australia Bank, 561 U.S., 472 (2010), which held that U.S. securities laws do not apply to securities that are not traded in the United States, even if the fraud occurs in the United States. In addition, some legal orders exert de facto external reach because they set standards for globally active actors. The "California effect" captures this neatly. It describes the effect of California's environmental standards on car makers in Illinois, which have little choice but to comply with California standards if they wish to sell their cars there. More recently, Anu Bradford has invoked the "Brussels Effect" to document the global impact of European law and, in part, of domestic choice-of-law rules, on international private law. Anu Bradford, *The Brussels Effect: How the European Union Rules the World* (Oxford: Oxford University Press, 2020).

17. Two entities have been critical for standardizing state law: the American Law Institute, a self-described "independent" organization founded in 1923, and the National Conference of State Legislatures, which has represented states in their pursuit of legal harmonization since its founding in 1975.

18. Richard M. Buxbaum and Klaus J. Hopt, *Legal Harmonization and the Business Enterprise* (Berlin: Walter de Gruyter, 1988). See also Johan de Bruycker, "EC Company Law—The European Company v. The European Economic Interest Grouping and the Harmonization of the National Company Laws," *Georgia Journal of International and Comparative Law* 21, no. 2 (1991): 191–216.

19. H. Patrick Glenn, "Harmonization of Law, Foreign Law and Private International Law," *European Review of Private Law* 1, no. 1/2 (1993): 47–66; Fabrizio Cafaggi and Horatia Muir-Watt, *Making European Private Law: Governance Design* (Cheltenham, U.K.: Edward Elgar, 2008); Willem H. van Boom, "Harmonizing Tort Law: A Comparative Tort Law and Economics Analysis," in *Tort Law and Economics*, ed. Michael Faure (Cheltenham, U.K.: Edward Elgar, 2009), 435–49.

20. Jean-Bernard Auby, "Is Legal Globalization Regulated? Memling and the Business of Baking Camels," *Utrecht Law Review* 4, no. 3 (2008): 210–17 (quote at 217).

21. The literature on legal pluralism has long made this point. See Sally Engle Merry, "Legal Pluralism," *Law & Society Review* 22, no. 5 (1988): 867–96. See also Breton et al., *Multijuralism*.

22. Claire Cutler, *Private Power and Global Authority: Transnational Merchant Law in the Global Political Economy* (Cambridge: Cambridge University Press, 2003); Hessel E. Yntema, "The Historic Bases of Private International Law," *American Journal of Comparative Law* 2, no. 3 (1953): 297–317.

23. Janet T. Landa, "A Theory of the Ethnically Homogeneous Middleman Group: An Institutional Alternative to Contract Law," *Journal of Legal Studies* 10, no. 2 (1981): 349–62; Avner Greif, "Reputation and Coalitions in Medieval Trade: Evidence on the Maghribi Traders," *Journal of Economic History* 59, no. 4 (1989): 857–82.

24. See, however, Lisa Bernstein, "Contract Governance in Small-World Networks: The Case of the Maghribi Traders," *Northwestern University Law Review* 113, no. 5 (2019): 1009–69.

25. Cutler, *Private Power and Global Authority;* Raymond de Roover, "Money, Banking, and Credit in Medieval Bruges," *Journal of Economic History* 2, no. S1 (1942): 52–65.

26. To the extent that the United States has standardized the law, it has used a soft-law approach.

27. Benito Arruñada, "Pitfalls to Avoid When Measuring the Institutional Environment: Is 'Doing Business' Damaging Business?," *Journal of Comparative Economics* 35, no. 4 (2007): 729–47.

28. Examples include the elections of Boris Johnson in the United Kingdom in 2019 following the Brexit vote, Donald Trump in the United States in 2016, and Narendra Modi in India in 2014.

29. For a summary and critique of these arguments, see Horatia Muir Watt, "Private International Law Beyond the Schism," *Transnational Legal Theory* 2, no. 3 (2011): 347–428. See also Hanoch Dagan and Sagi Peari, "Choice of Law Meets Private Law Theory," *Oxford Journal of Legal Studies* 43, no. 3 (2023): 520–45.

30. See, however, Clayton Gillette and Robert E. Scott, "The Political Economy of International Sales Law," *International Review of Law and Economics* 25, no. 3 (2005): 446–86.

31. For a summary of relevant case law, see Harold Horowitz, "The Commerce Clause as a Limitation on State Choice-of-Law Doctrine," *Harvard Law Review* 84, no. 4 (1971): 806–24. The Constitution's "full faith and credit" clause is more typically associated with ensuring that each state respects the others' laws. U.S. Constitution, art. IV, sec. 1.

32. Samuel S. Arsht, "A History of Delaware Corporation Law," *Delaware Journal of Corporate Law* 1, no. 1 (1976): 1–22; William J. Carney, George B. Shepherd, and Joanna Shepherd, "Lawyers, Ignorance, and the Dominance of Delaware Corporate Law," *Harvard Business Law Review* 2, no. 1 (2012): 124–51; Jill E. Fisch, "The Peculiar Role of the Delaware Courts in the Competition for Corporate Charters," *University of Cincinnati Law Review* 68, no. 4 (2000): 1061–100; Mark Roe, "Delaware's Politics," *Harvard Law Review* 118, no. 8 (2005): 2491.

33. Marcel Kahan and Ehud Kamar, "The Myth of State Competition in Corporate Law," *Stanford Law Review* 55, no. 3 (2002): 679.

34. Sujeet Indap, "The Battle Over Who Makes the Rules for U.S. Companies," *Financial Times*, August 5, 2024.

35. Efraim Benmelech and Tobias J. Moskowitz, "The Political Economy of Financial Regulation: Evidence from U.S. State Usury Laws in the 19th Century," *Journal of Finance* 65, no. 3 (2010): 1029–73; Steven Mercatante, "The Deregulation of Usury Ceilings, Rise of Easy Credit, and Increasing Consumer Debt," *South Dakota Law Review* 53, no. 1 (2008): 37–51.

36. Jamie Smyth, " 'Texas Two-Step': The U.S. Legal Move Letting Corporations Off the Hook," *Financial Times*, October 25, 2022.

37. Werner F. Ebke, "*Centros*—Some Realities and Some Mysteries," *American Journal of Comparative Law* 48, no. 4 (2000): 623–60; Eddy Wymeersch, "Centros: A Landmark Decision in European Company Law,"

in *Corporations, Capital Markets and Business in the Law*, ed. Theodor Baums, Klaus J. Hopt, and Norbert Horn (London: Kluwer Law International, 2000), 629–54.

38. Carsten Gerner-Beuerle and Federico Mucciarelli, "Cross-Border Reincorporations in the European Union: The Case for Comprehensive Harmonisation," *Journal of Corporate Law Studies* 18, no. 1 (2018): 1–42.

39. Klaus J. Hopt, "Labor Representation on Corporate Boards: Impacts and Problems for Corporate Governance and Economic Integration in Europe," *International Review of Law and Economics* 14, no. 2 (1994): 203–14. See also Pistor, "Codetermination."

40. See Benjamin Fuhrmann, "Corporate Law Competition in the EU Revisited: Italian Corporations Moving North and the Missing German SPACs," *Columbia Journal of Transnational Law* (forthcoming).

41. "SPACs—Alternative Form of Financing and Investment," Börse Frankfurt, https://www.boerse-frankfurt.de/en/spacs.

42. Carney, Shepherd, and Shepherd, "Lawyers, Ignorance, and the Dominance of Delaware Corporate Law."

43. Robert Daines, "The Incorporation Choices of IPO Firms," *NYU Law Review* 77, no. 6 (2002): 1559–611. In the United States, all major law schools teach (exclusively) Delaware corporate law. It is also the law that foreign students learn when studying for their master's in the United States.

44. See also Pistor, *The Code of Capital*, chaps. 6 and 7.

45. See Michaels, "Der Code des Kapitals und seiner Portabilität." Michaels applauds the fact that in my previous book I put conflict-of-law rules on the table for future reforms, but argues (correctly) that future reforms should not be limited to choice-of-law rules alone.

46. This is the default rule under article 4 of Regulation No. 864/2007 of the European Parliament and of the Council of 11 July 2007 on the Law Applicable to Non-Contractual Obligations ("Rome II"), available at http://data.europa.eu/eli/reg/2007/864/oj.

47. See recital 25 of Rome II.

48. "Community policy on the environment shall aim at a high level of protection taking into account the diversity of situations in the various regions of the Community. It shall be based on the precautionary principle and on the principles that preventive action should be taken, that environmental damage should as a priority be rectified at source and that the polluter should pay." Article 174(2) of the EU Treaty.

49. On precarity, rather than inequality, as the true cause of capitalism's fragility, see Azmanova, *Capitalism on Edge*.

50. Robert Wai, "Transnational Liftoff and Juridical Touchdown: The Regulatory Function of Private International Law in an Era of Globalization," *Columbia Journal of Transnational Law* 40, no. 2 (2002): 209.

51. Meinhard v. Salmon, 249 N.Y. 458, 464 (1928).

52. John C. Coffee, "The Mandatory/Enabling Balance in Corporate Law: An Essay on the Judicial Role," *Columbia Law Review* 89, no. 7 (1989): 1618–91.

53. See sections 102(b)(7) and 122(17) of the Delaware General Corporation Law.

54. According to Delaware's limited partnership law, "duties may be expanded or restricted or eliminated by provisions in the partnership agreement." Del. Code Ann. tit. 6, § 17-1101(d). A similar provision can be found in section 1101 of Delaware's limited liability company statute, see Del. Code Ann. tit. 6, § 18-1101. Both statutes are available at www.delcode.delaware.gov. See also New Enterprise Associates v. Rich, 295 A.3d. 520, 574 (Del. Ch. 2023).

55. For example, victims of sex trafficking or labor trafficking may apply for a T visa. See 8 C.F.R. § 241.11 (2023). Recent Department of Homeland Security guidance allows undocumented immigrants who are witnesses to potential labor-law violations to apply for deferred action. See "DHS Support of the Enforcement of Labor and Employment Laws," U.S. Citizenship and Immigration Services, accessed April 24, 2024, https://www.uscis.gov/working-in-the-united-states/information-for-employers-and-employees/dhs-support-of-the-enforcement-of-labor-and-employment-laws; Hoffman Plastic Compounds, Inc. v. NLRB, 122 S. Ct. 1275 (2002). In the wake of *Hoffman Plastics*, the Department of Labor issued guidance that it will continue to enforce the Fair Labor Standards Act without regard to the victim's immigration status, reasoning that for minimum-wage or overtime violations, for example, *Hoffman Plastics*' prohibition on back pay "for years of work not performed, for wages that could not lawfully have been earned" does not apply to nonpayment for work actually performed. "Application of U.S. Labor Laws to Immigrant Workers: Effect of Hoffman Plastics Decision on Laws Enforced by the Wage and Hour Division," Fact Sheet No. 48, U.S. Department of Labor, Wage and Hour Division, revised July 2008, https://www.dol.gov/agencies/whd/fact-sheets/48-hoffman-plastics.

56. Harold Meyerson, "How the American South Drives the Low-Wage Economy," *American Prospect*, July 6, 2015. A countermovement is under way, however. See Luke Goldstein, "Has Organized Labor Finally Cracked the South?," *American Prospect*, May 29, 2024.

57. Dagan and Peari, "Choice of Law Meets Private Law Theory."

58. Roberta Romano, "Empowering Investors: A Market Approach to Securities Regulation," *Yale Law Journal* 107, no. 8 (1998): 2359–430.

59. Merritt B. Fox, "Retaining Mandatory Securities Disclosure: Why Issuer Choice Is Not Investor Empowerment," *Virginia Law Review* 85, no. 7 (1999): 1335–419; Merritt Fox, "The Issuer Choice Debate," *Theoretical Inquires in Law* 2, no. 2 (2001): 563–611. See also John C. Coates, "Private vs. Political Choice of Securities Regulation: A Political Cost/Benefit Analysis," *Virginia Journal of International Law* 41, no. 3 (2001): 531–82.

60. For details, see the discussion in the following chapter.

61. See Dagan and Peari, "Choice of Law Meets Private Theory," 534. Their argument can be read to go even further, but it ignores the difficulty of enforcing these inherent limitations. More on this in the final two chapters of the book.

62. Tony and Cherie Blair avoided paying the stamp duty by buying an offshore shell company that held the property in London that they wished to acquire. See "Pandora Papers: Secret Wealth and Dealings of World Leaders Exposed," *BBC News,* October 3, 2021, https://www.bbc.co.uk/news/world-58780465.

63. Helvering v. Gregory, 69 F.2d 809 (2d Cir. 1934). Professor Marvin A. Chirelstein characterized Judge Hand's decision as "a major event in the history of tax administration." Marvin A. Chirelstein, "Learned Hand's Contribution to the Law of Tax Avoidance," *Yale Law Journal* 77, no. 3 (1968): 441.

64. As discussed in chapter 1, the rule of law is a deeply, or essentially, contested concept. Jeremy Waldron, "Is the Rule of Law Essentially a Contested Concept (in Florida)?," *Law and Philosophy* 21, no. 2 (2002): 137–64. Defining it may be difficult, but for it to remain essentially contested, it must have a broader appeal than simply serving as an instrument in the pursuit of private wealth.

Chapter 6. Rewiring the System

1. Andre Gunder Frank, *Capitalism and Underdevelopment in Latin America: Historical Studies of Chile and Brazil* (New York: Monthly Review Press, 1967).

2. Frank, *Capitalism and Underdevelopment in Latin America,* 116–17.

3. Frank, *Capitalism and Underdevelopment in Latin America,* 120.

4. Joanna Kusiak, "Trespassing on the Law: Critical Legal Engineering as a Strategy for Action Research," *Area* (Royal Geographical Society) 53, no. 4 (2021): 603–10 (quote at 605).

5. Kusiak, "Trespassing on the Law."

6. Joanna Kusiak, *Radically Legal: Berlin Constitutes the Future* (Cambridge: Cambridge University Press, 2024).

7. See also my critique of materialist arguments in chapter 2.

8. Etymology: Origin of the Word, https://etymology.net/crisis.

9. John F. Padgett, "Country as Global Market: Netherlands, Calvinism, and the Joint Stock Company," in John F. Padgett and Walter W. Powell, *The Emergence of Organizations and Markets* (Princeton, N.J.: Princeton University Press, 2012), 208–34.

10. Padgett, "Country as Global Market," 231.

11. Padgett, "Country as Global Market."

12. On the corporate-law innovations of the Dutch East India Company (VOC), see Guiseppe Dari-Matiacci et al., "The Emergence of the Corporate Form," *Journal of Law, Economics & Organization* 33, no. 2 (2016): 193–236.

13. Dari-Matiacci et al., "The Emergence of the Corporate Form."

14. For an excellent account of the crisis, see Tooze, *Crashed*.

15. The mechanism is the expansion of humans into the habitat of wild animals, which makes it more likely that viruses will find their way from them to humans. Whether this is how the Covid pandemic originated remains disputed. See Mariana Lenharo and Lauren Wolf, "U.S. Covid-Origins Hearing Renews Debate over Lab-Leak Hypothesis," *Nature*, March 9, 2023.

16. These crises include the run on U.S. treasuries in the spring of 2020 at the beginning of the Covid crisis, the turbulence in U.K. financial markets in 2022, and the failure of Silicon Valley Bank and several others in the spring of 2023. For an analysis of the post-Covid financial crises in the United States, including the collapse of Silicon Valley Bank, see Ben Spies-Butcher and Gareth Bryant, "The History and Future of the Tax State: Possibilities for a New Fiscal Politics Beyond Neoliberalism," *Critical Perspectives on Accounting* 98 (2024). For an analysis of the U.K. financial crisis, see Ethan Ilzetzki, "UK Financial Crisis of 2022: Retrospective Diagnosis and Policy Recommendations," CFM Discussion Paper No. 2024-08, London School of Economics Centre for Macroeconomics, February 2024), https://www.lse.ac.uk/CFM/assets/pdf/CFM-Discussion-Papers-2024/CFMDP2024-08-Paper.pdf. Precipitating this polycrisis, however, was a broader global financial instability that some commentators have traced back to the growth of repurchase agreements, or repos. See Carolyn Sissoko, "Repurchase Agreements and the De(con)struction of Financial Markets," *Economy and Society* 48, no. 3 (2019): 315–41.

17. This has been most evident in the case of the rescue of the customers of Silicon Valley Bank in 2023, who had opted against insured deposits and for uninsured accounts in order to obtain higher returns, yet successfully sought protection from the U.S. Treasury when this scheme (predictably) imploded. Pete Schroeder, "After Silicon Valley Bank's Shutdown, Uninsured Depositors Face Tense Wait," *Reuters,* March 10, 2023; Federal Deposit Insurance Corporation, "FDIC Acts to Protect All Depositors of the Former Silicon Valley Bank, Santa Clara, California," press release, March 13, 2023, https://www.fdic.gov/news/press-releases/2023/pr23019.html.

18. On the hybridity of money and finance, see Perry Mehrling, "Essential Hybridity: A Money View of Law and Finance for Foreign Exchange," *Journal of Comparative Economics* 41, no. 2 (2013): 355–63.

19. For details of this metaphor developed by Poulantzas, see chapter 2.

20. The United States passed the Coronavirus Aid, Relief, and Economic Security (CARES) Act in March 2020 and the Coronavirus Response and Consolidated Appropriations Act in December 2020, which provided $2.2 trillion and $900 billion, respectively, in stimulus spending for individuals, small businesses, and others. In the European Union, the European Commission's NextGenerationEU (NextGenEU) allocated €806.9 billion toward Covid-19 recovery efforts.

21. Jeremy Roos, *Why Not Default? The Political Economy of Sovereign Debt* (Princeton, N.J.: Princeton University Press, 2019); Julian Schumacher, Christoph Trebesch, and Henrik Enderlein, "What Explains Sovereign Debt Litigation," *Journal of Law and Economics* 58, no. 3 (2015): 585–623.

22. Maurice Obstfeld, Jay C. Shambaugh, and Allen M. Taylor, "Financial Instability, Reserves, and Central Bank Swap Lines in the Panic of 2008," *American Economic Review* 99, no. 2 (2009): 480–86; Stijn Claessens et al., "Lessons and Policy Implications from the Global Financial Crisis," Working Paper No. 2010/44 (International Monetary Fund, February 2010); Ana Santos Rutschman, "Intellectual Property Protections for Vaccines and PPE," in *Outsmarting the Next Pandemic: What Covid-19 Can Teach Us,* ed. Elizabeth Kirley and Deborah Porter (Abingdon, U.K.: Routledge, 2022), 169–89.

23. In December 2023, the U.S. Fed announced that interest rate decreases were on the horizon for 2024. Colby Smith and Claire Jones, "Federal Reserve Triggers Market Rally as It Signals Interest Rate Cuts in 2024," *Financial Times,* December 14, 2023.

24. Milton Friedman, *Inflation: Causes and Consequences* (London: Asia Publishing House, 1963). The economist Isabella Weber has proffered one

such critique in advocating for strategic price controls as a check on inflation, which triggered substantial and at times rancorous debate. Isabella Weber, "Could Strategic Price Controls Help Fight Inflation?," *Guardian*, December 29, 2021.

25. Isabella M. Weber et al., "Inflation in Times of Overlapping Emergencies: Systemically Significant Prices from an Input-Output Perspective," *Industrial and Corporate Change* 33, no. 2 (2024): 297–341.

26. Not all have stayed. Donald Trump was voted out of office after only one term, but was elected president again in 2024; in Poland, the Law and Justice Party had to yield to the return of Donald Tusk; and the United Kingdom's experience with Brexit has somewhat dampened the enthusiasm for others (such as Italy, France, or the Netherlands) to follow. Still, even in countries where populists were voted out of office, elections have been close, and politics remain deeply contested.

27. This is evidenced in surveys about trust in the existing system. See, for example, the Edelman Trust Barometer, https://www.edelman.com/trust/2021-trust-barometer.

28. Karl Polanyi, "History in the Gear of Social Change," in *The Great Transformation*, 245–56.

29. For details, see chapter 2.

30. Graeber, *Debt: The First 5,000 Years*.

31. See Pistor, *The Code of Capital*, chap. 4.

32. This money view of finance is inspired by Minsky but fully developed in Mehrling, *The New Lombard Street*.

33. Victor Mayer-Schönberger and Kenneth Cukier, *Big Data: A Revolution That Will Transform How We Live and Think* (Boston: Houghton Mifflin Harcourt, 2013).

34. Frank, *Capitalism and Underdevelopment in Latin America*.

35. Niklas Luhmann, *Law as a Social System* (Oxford: Oxford University Press, 2008). The book was translated by Klaus A. Ziegert from the original German, which was published in 1993.

36. This theory has been effectively critiqued by others. See, for example, Rainer Greshoff, "Ohne Akteure geht es nicht! Oder: Warum die Fundamente der Luhmannschen Sozialtheorie nicht tragen" [It will not work without actors! or: Why the foundations of Luhmann's social theory are unsustainable], *Zeitschrift für Soziologie* 37, no. 6 (2008): 450–69; Alex Viskovatoff, "Foundations of Niklas Luhmann's Theory of Social Systems," *Philosophy of the Social Sciences* 29, no. 4 (1999): 481–516.

37. Luhmann, *Law as a Social System*, 128.

38. Luhmann, *Law as a Social System*, 252.

39. Luhmann, *Law as a Social System*, 347.

40. See also the discussion of incremental, yet transformative, change in chapter 5.

41. Luhmann, *Law as a Social System*, 401.

42. Lawrence Lessig, *Code and Other Laws of Cyberspace* (New York: Basic Books, 1999), chaps. 1, 3.

43. Narendar Pani, "Historical Origins of Modern Corruption: The Making of the Gap Between Legality and Morality in Bangalore" (unpublished manuscript, 2014) (on file with author).

44. Olivier Nay, "Fragile Failed States: Critical Perspectives on Conceptual Hybrids," *International Political Science Review* 34, no. 3 (2013): 326–41; Michael W. Doyle and Nicholas Sambanis, *Making War and Building Peace* (Princeton, N.J.: Princeton University Press, 2006). Doyle and Sambanis point out that any lasting peace requires a minimum consensus among the formerly warring parties.

Chapter 7. Beyond Capitalist Law

1. Minsky used the term "survival constraint" to describe what Janos Kornai later called a "budget constraint." Both argued that in principle private actors operate under a hard constraint, whereas state-owned or state-sponsored entities operate under a soft survival or budget constraint. Minsky, *Stabilizing an Unstable Economy;* Janos Kornai, Eric Maskin, and Roland Gerard, "Understanding the Soft Budget Constraint," *Journal of Economic Literature* 41, no. 4 (2003): 1095–136.

2. Eric Maskin, "The Soft Budget Constraint," *American Economic Review* 89, no. 2 (1999): 421–25.

3. Tobias Adrian and Hyun Song Shin, "The Shadow Banking System: Implications for Financial Regulation," Staff Report No. 389 (Federal Reserve Bank of New York, July 2009); Zoltan Pozsar and Manmohan Singh, "The Nonbank-Bank Nexus and the Shadow Banking System," Working Paper No. 2011/289 (International Monetary Fund, December 2011).

4. Martin Arnold and Costas Mourselas, "Top ECB Official Sounds Alarm on Rising Risks from Shadow Banking," *Financial Times*, July 10, 2024.

5. Dagan, *A Liberal Theory of Property;* Martijn W. Hesselink, *Justifying Contract in Europe: Political Philosophies of European Contract Law* (Oxford: Oxford University Press, 2020). See also Hanoch Dagan and Benjamin C. Zipursky, *Research Handbook on Private Law Theory* (Cheltenham, U.K.: Edward Elgar Publishing, 2020).

6. Roman law and, following it, civil-law systems like to define property rights as an absolute right in the sense that they confer powers against anyone, not just against specific parties with whom there is a contractual or

similar legal relation. It is a right *in rem*, not just *in personam*. However, this does not exclude the possibility of legal limits to property rights, including in private law itself, such as sharing mandates for marital property and mandatory licensing requirements for intellectual property rights. See Dagan, "Inside Property."

7. Neil Komesar, *Law's Limits: The Rule of Law and the Supply and Demand of Rights* (Cambridge: Cambridge University Press, 2001).

8. For a summary of this point of view and critique thereof, see Hesselink, *Justifying Contract in Europe*, 75.

9. Hesselink, *Justifying Contract in Europe*, 142.

10. See, however, Dagan and Dorfman, "The Human Right to Private Property."

11. Grewal, *Network Power*, 106–11.

12. Martijn W. Hesselink, "Reconstituting the Code of Capital: Could a Progressive European Code of Private Law Help Us Reduce Inequality and Regain Democratic Control?," *European Law Open* 1, no. 2 (2022): 316–43 (quote at 323).

13. Several attempts at creating a European code have been abandoned after years of trying. Ruth Sefton-Green, "Les Codes manqués," *Revue trimestrielle de droit civil* 2005, no. 3 (2005): 539–47; Martijn W. Hesselink, "The Politics of a European Civil Code," *European Law Journal* 10, no. 6 (2004): 675.

14. Hesselink, "Reconstituting the Code of Capital," 327.

15. As Luhmann wrote, "A clear division between justice and moral judgment and ethical reflection is not only a matter of the autonomy of the legal system. It also guarantees that a moral judgment on law can be made independently from law." Luhmann, *Law as a Social System*, 225.

16. Luhmann, *Law as a Social System*, 338.

17. Katharina Pistor, "Legal Coding Beyond Capital," *European Law Open* 1, no. 2 (2022): 344–50.

18. Brishen Rogers, "The Law and Political Economy of Workplace Technological Change," *Harvard Civil Rights–Civil Liberties Law Review* 55, no. 2 (2020): 532–84.

19. Hélène Landemore, *Open Democracy: Reinventing Popular Rule for the Twenty-First Century* (Princeton, N.J.: Princeton University Press, 2020). In this book, Landemore develops the principles for constituting a statistically representative cross section of the entire population for constitution making.

20. Amartya Sen, *Commodities and Capabilities* (Amsterdam: North Holland, 1985); Martha Nussbaum, *Creating Capabilities: The Human Development Approach* (Cambridge, Mass.: Belknap Press of Harvard University Press, 2011).

21. On the potential of moderate reforms to create a "magnet effect" for social transformation, see Aldashev et al., "Formal Law as a Magnet to Reform Custom."

22. A voluminous literature has critiqued rights-based approaches theoretically as well as in domestic and international law. See Greene, *How Rights Went Wrong*; Moyn, *Not Enough*; Menke, *Critique of Rights*.

23. Sen, *Commodities and Capabilities*.

24. Sen, *Commodities and Capabilities*, 1.

25. Sen, *Commodities and Capabilities* 3.

26. Sen, *Commodities and Capabilities*, 3 (emphasis added).

27. Sen, *Commodities and Capabilities*, 19.

28. Amartya K. Sen, *Development as Freedom* (New York: Random House, 1999), chap. 3 (esp. p. 54).

29. Nussbaum, *Creating Capabilities*, 295. She advocates expanding the approach to nonhuman animals as well.

30. Nussbaum, *Creating Capabilities*, 297.

31. For details, see the discussion below.

32. Nussbaum, *Creating Capabilities*, 280. See also Martha Nussbaum, *Women and Human Development: The Capabilities Approach* (Cambridge: Cambridge University Press, 2000).

33. For an account of how U.S. law has treated women and children in comparison with household animals, see Claire Priest, "Enforcing Sympathy: Animal Cruelty Doctrine After the Civil War," *Law & Social Inquiry* 44, no. 1 (2019): 136–69.

34. Nussbaum, *Creating Capabilities*, 280.

35. Nussbaum, *Creating Capabilities*, 280.

36. Martha Nussbaum, "Capabilities as Fundamental Entitlements: Sen and Social Justice," *Feminist Economics* 9, nos. 2–3 (2003): 33–59. See also Nussbaum, *Creating Capabilities*.

37. Capability 10 in the catalogue. See Nussbaum, "Capabilities as Fundamental Entitlements," 42.

38. Nussbaum, "Capabilities as Fundamental Entitlements," 42.

39. Nussbaum, "Capabilities as Fundamental Entitlements," 42.

40. The Ten Principles of the UN Global Compact, https://unglobal-compact.org/what-is-gc/mission/principles. John Ruggie was instrumental in developing the ideas for these principles. See John G. Ruggie, "Business and Human Rights: Mapping International Standards of Responsibility and Accountability for Corporate Acts," U.N. Document A/HRC/4/35 (United Nations, February 19, 2007).

41. "New Report Shows Just 100 Companies Are Source of over 70% of Emissions," CDP Worldwide, July 10, 2017, https://www.cdp.net/en/

articles/media/new-report-shows-just-100-companies-are-source-of-over-70-of-emissions.

42. Nassim Nicholas Taleb, Rupert Read, and Raphael Douady, "The Precautionary Principle (with Application to the Genetic Modification of Organisms)," NYU School of Engineering Working Paper Series, 2014, www.fooledbyrandomness.com/pp2.pdf.

43. For its application to financial policy, see Hugues Chenet, Josh Ryan-Collins, and Frank van Lerven, "Finance, Climate-Change and Radical Uncertainty: Towards a Precautionary Approach to Financial Policy," *Ecological Economics* 183 (2021): 1–14.

44. Section 402A of the Restatement (Second) of Torts. See also Peter Cane, "Deterrence and Strict Liability for Defective Products in the United Kingdom," *Journal of Products Liability* 3, no. 3 (1979): 135. In Europe, the same principles have been codified in the product-liability directive, available at http://data.europa.eu/eli/dir/1985/374/oj.

45. Sections 11 and 12 of the Securities Act of 1933, available at https://www.law.cornell.edu/wex/securities_act_of_1933. Under the "fraud on the market" doctrine, it is enough for investors to show that prices changed and that they bought or sold a security, not that they actually listened to misleading information. See Basic, Inc. v. Levinson, 485 U.S. 224 (1998).

46. Harold Demsetz, "Toward a Theory of Property Rights," *American Economic Review* 57, no. 2 (1967): 347–59; Louis De Alessi, "Property Rights, Transaction Costs, and X-Efficiency: An Essay in Economic Theory," *American Economic Review* 73, no. 1 (1983): 64–81.

47. See chapter 3.

48. Zuckerberg said, "Unless you are breaking stuff, you are not moving fast enough." Henry Blodget, "Mark Zuckerberg On Innovation," *Business Insider,* October 1, 2009.

49. Sandra K. Miller, "Piercing the Corporate Veil Among Affiliated Companies in the European Community and in the U.S.: A Comparative Analysis of U.S., German, and U.K. Veil-Piercing Approaches," *American Business Law Journal* 36, no. 1 (1998): 73–149; Robert Thompson, "Piercing the Corporate Veil: An Empirical Study," *Cornell Law Review* 76, no. 5 (1991): 1036–74. But see Stephen M. Bainbridge, "Abolishing Veil Piercing," *Journal of Corporation Law* 26, no. 3 (2001): 479–535.

50. Shmuel I. Becher and Uri Benoliel, "Dark Contracts," *Boston College Law Review* 64, no. 1 (2023): 55–117.

51. The "clean hands" doctrine "closes the doors of a court of equity to one tainted with inequitableness or bad faith relative to the matter in

which he seeks relief, however improper may have been the behavior of the defendant." Precision Instrument Manufacturing Co. v. Automotive Maintenance Machinery Co., 324 U.S. 806, 814 (1945). The underlying normative principle is that a plaintiff who has himself not acted in good faith should not be able to then run to the courts for recourse; it is akin to a loss of standing. See also Ori J. Herstein, "A Normative Theory of the Clean Hands Defense," *Legal Theory* 17, no. 3 (2011): 171–208.

52. Cohen, *Between Truth and Power*.

53. Guiseppe Dari-Matiacci and Carmine Guerriero, "Law and Culture: A Theory of Comparative Variation in Bona Fide Purchase Rules," *Oxford Journal of Legal Studies* 35, no. 3 (2015): 543–74.

54. Article 11 of Directive 2004/25/EC of the European Parliament and of the Council of 21 April 2004 on Takeover Bids.

55. Nussbaum argues that the capabilities approach "supplies a threshold of adequacy." Nussbaum, *Creating Capabilities*, 295.

56. The favored term of Germany's former minister of finance to ensure a balanced budget. See " 'Father of the Black Zero': Germany's Love Affair with Austerity," *Deutsche Welle (DW)*, December 27, 2023, available at www.dw.com.

57. Perry Mehrling, "The Inherent Hierarchy of Money," in *Social Fairness and Economics: Economic Essays in the Spirit of Duncan Foley*, ed. Lance Taylor, Armon Rezai, and Thomas Michl (New York: Routledge, 2012), 394–404. For a critique of Mehrling, see Kapadia, *A Political Theory of Money*.

58. Hyman P. Minsky, *Can "It" Happen Again? Essays on Instability and Finance* (Armonk, N.Y.: Sharpe, 1982). For a lucid explanation of Minsky's thinking, see Mehrling, "The Vision of Hyman P. Minsky."

59. Mehrling, "The Inherent Hierarchy of Money."

60. Hockett and Omarova, "The Finance Franchise."

61. Christine Desan, "The Monetary Structure of Economic Activity: A Constitutional Analysis," *Law and Contemporary Problems* 86, no. 4 (2024): 77–110. See also Desan, *Making Money*.

62. A classic is Silvio Gesell, *Die Natürliche Wirtschaftsordnung* (Nürnberg: Rudolf Zitzmann Verlag, 1949). For more recent accounts, see Bernard Lietaer and Jacqui Dunne, *Rethinking Money: How New Currencies Turn Scarcity into Prosperity* (San Francisco: Berrett-Koehler Publishers, 2013).

63. Robert Hockett and Aaron James, *Money from Nothing—Or Why We Should Stop Worrying About Debt and Love the Federal Reserve* (Brooklyn, N.Y.: Melville House Publishing, 2020).

Epilogue

1. Financial and economic meltdowns have caused political regime change in the past, including in Germany in the 1930s and Indonesia in the 1990s.
2. North, *Institutions, Institutional Change, and Economic Performance*, 7.
3. Hodgson, "On the Institutional Foundations of Law" (arguing that law can be sustained only when it is commensurate with informal institutions).
4. Alexander Borsa et al., "Evaluating Trends in Private Equity Ownership and Impacts on Health Outcomes, Costs, and Quality: Systematic Review," *BMJ*, no. 382 (2023), https://doi.org/10.1136/bmj-2023-075244.

Index

Alito, Samuel, 70–71
alternative dispute resolution (ADR), 78–79
Althusser, Louis, 27
Amazon, 64
American Law Institute, 173n17
anarchy, 115
Anderson, Elizabeth, 9–10
Anthropocene, 5
arbitrage. *See* legal arbitrage
arbitration, 76–79, 134
Arendt, Hannah, 128
artificial intelligence (AI), 45
assets. *See* financial assets
Auby, Jean-Bernard, 90
Auer, Marietta, 49–50
autonomy. *See* individual autonomy

banks/banking, 106–8, 118, 136–37
Becker, Gary, 44
Bill of Rights. *See* U.S. Bill of Rights
Black, Hugo, 35
Black populations, 35, 58–59, 72–73
Blackstone, William, 59, 120
Blair, Tony, 99, 177n62
Bradford, Anu, 172n16
breakthrough rule, 134
Bretton Woods system, 8
Brussels effect, 172n16

Calabresi, Guido, 53–54
California, 132
California effect, 172n16

capabilities approach. *See* human capabilities approach
capitalism: appropriation of collective resources by, 2; center-periphery structure of, 102–3, 107, 111; colonialism fueled by, 6; constituting/reconstituting of, by legal means, ix, 8, 12–13, 38–39; constraints on, ix, 8–9, 11–13, 22, 40; contradictions of, 5; coordinated vs. liberal, 62–63; core logic of, 2, 142; critiques of, 16–18, 27, 40, 103, 109; defenses of, 3; democracy in relation to, 22, 35; expansionist nature of, 39–40; externalities of, 8; fragility of, 23; hierarchies of power fundamental to, 34–35; legal regime of, 1–7, 10–11, 23, 37–39, 102, 109–13, 117, 137–39; meanings of the term, 2; modern state coextensive with, 5–6, 11; and nature, 3, 5, 39–40, 102; property rights linked to, 45; reform of, x, 3–4, 19, 38, 40, 102–38, 142–43; social/global problems arising from, 3; transition from socialism to, 21–22; understanding of, 1–2; United States and United Kingdom as exemplars of, 7, 9, 22, 57, 62, 95, 106; use of the law by, ix–x. *See also* economy/market

187

capitalist law: core features of, 7,
    11–12, 141; internationalism of,
    7, 11; legal arbitrage within, 89,
    99–101; private interests
    prioritized over public interests
    by, 2–4, 6, 11, 16, 22–23, 117,
    139; as a productive force, 38–39;
    and property, 49–50; reform of, x,
    3–4, 8, 38, 40, 102–38, 142–43;
    theories of, 21–30, 37–38;
    vulnerabilities of, 104; who
    benefits from, 102. *See also* legal
    empowerment; private law
Cardozo, Benjamin, 97
care, duty of. *See* duty of care
central banks, 1, 106–8, 118,
    136–37
Chile, 64
Chirelstein, Marvin A., 177n63
choice of law/forum, 76, 89, 93–99,
    134, 175n45
citizen tribunals, 123, 130
civil law, 24, 29, 70, 73–75, 77, 95,
    123, 181n6
class-action suits, 73–75
clean hands doctrine, 133, 184n51
climate change, 3, 5, 45, 106, 109,
    115, 130–31. *See also* nature
Coase, Ronald, 34, 161n45
Coase theorem, 33, 50, 161n45
coercion, powers of legal, 66–82;
    arbitration and, 76–79;
    globalized markets and, 75–79;
    legitimacy of, 28, 66; means of
    access to, 71–72, 77–79, 82, 123,
    140; private actors' access to, ix, 3,
    11–13, 67, 69–75, 79, 82, 140;
    socialization of the cost of,
    79–80; state's command of, 11,
    28, 41, 66. *See also* litigation
Coffee, Jack, 97

Cohen, G. A., 38
colonialism and post-colonialism,
    6, 56–57
comity, 89
commerce clause, of U.S. Constitution, 93
commodification, of humans,
    society, and law, 25–26
Commodity Futures Modernization Act (2000), 69
common law, 24, 29, 53, 67, 69, 95,
    124
Commons, John, 17, 27, 29
communism, 7, 19, 22, 108
comparative law, 24
compensation, 52–53
conflict of laws, 76, 91–92, 140
Consumer Financial Protection
    Bureau (CFPB), 78
consumer-protection laws, 169n41
contracts: asymmetry of power in,
    11, 61, 65, 81–82, 119; consent
    assumed for, 43, 60, 119, 133;
    consumer financial, 78; dark, 133;
    democratization of, 120; digitized
    (smart), 81–82; domination by
    means of, 60–65, 113; evolution
    of law and, 42; incompleteness of,
    84; labor, 61–64; moral scruples
    about, 69; property compared to,
    60; "take responsibility" principle
    for, 133–34
Cornell, Nicolas, 81
corporations: class-action suits
    against, 73–75; defined, 34;
    Delaware laws concerning,
    93–94, 97, 175n43; in European
    Union, 94; Fourteenth Amendment employed in service of, 35;
    legal empowerment of, 10–11,
    68; liability protection granted to,

45–46, 54, 132–33; migration of, 98; personal rights granted to, 14, 34, 35, 73, 126, 133; shareholders' rights and responsibilities, 45–46, 49, 54, 132–33, 139. *See also* multinational corporations
courts. *See* coercion, powers of legal; litigation
Covid pandemic, 106–8, 135, 142
crises, change arising from, 104–6
critical legal studies, 36

Dagan, Hanoch, 10–11, 98–99
dark contracts, 133
data: as an asset, 38; European Union laws on, 60; individuals' production of, 45, 49, 65, 133; individuals' right to, 69–70; as property, 45, 49, 65, 70, 133–34
debt, 42, 81
Declaration of the Rights of Man and of the Citizen (France, 1789), 44
Delaware, corporate law in, 93–94, 97, 175n43
democracy: capitalism in relation to, 22, 35; legal policies in service of, x–xi, 4, 23, 33, 35, 77, 95–97, 116, 120–25, 137; norms of, 14–15, 33, 35; populism and, 5, 22, 108
derivatives, 69, 114
digital platforms, 60–61
Dingell, John, 79
discovery, 75
do-it-yourself (DIY) law, 90, 95, 97
domination: contracts as means of, 60–65; law as means of, 28, 36; private law used for, 2, 119–21; property as means of, 59. *See also* power
Dorfman, Avihay, 10–11

Dutch East India Company, 105
duty of care, 55, 132–33

ecocide, 3
economy/market: globalized, 75–79; human capabilities approach and, 126; neutrality imputed to, 33; public law's role in development and maintenance of, 117–18; the state in relation to, 5–6, 17, 21–22, 29–30, 32–33. *See also* capitalism
Energy Charter Treaty, 59
Engels, Friedrich, 5, 16, 24, 45
England, 29, 52–53
English East India Corporation, 56
Enlightenment, 15, 49
enumeration principle, 48–49
environmental, social, and governance (ESG) investing, 59, 163n75
EPL-code, 121, 123, 182n13
European Union (EU): and alternative dispute resolution, 78–79; and choice of law, 93–94, 96; consumer-protection laws in, 169n41; corporate law in, 94; data laws of, 60; free movement of labor in, 62–63; harmonization of laws in, 89, 92–93, 96; labor laws in, 165n97; as a leading capitalist economy, 106; populist hostility toward, 22; private-law code for, 121, 123, 182n13; Treaty of, 96

Facebook, 132
failed states, 66, 115
Fair Credit Reporting Act (1970), 71
Fair Labor Standards Act (1938), 113

family, law related to, 24, 67–68
fascism, 22, 27, 108
Federal Arbitration Act (1925), 77–78
Federal Rules of Civil Procedure, 74, 75, 79
fiduciary duties, 97–98, 132
financial assets: debt as, 42; legal nature of, 8; as property, 46, 49
financial system, 117–18
Finland, 64
foreign direct investment, 63
Foucault, Michel, 27, 32
Fourteenth Amendment, 35, 73
Fox, Merritt, 98–99
France, 29, 61, 94
franchises, 76
Frank, Andre Gunder, 102–3, 111
Friedman, Milton, 107

Galanter, Marc, 43, 62
Germany, 47–48, 68–69, 94–95
ghost work, 63, 64
Ginsburg, Ruth Bader, 71
Glass-Steagall Act (1933), 113
Gray, Mary, 64
Great Depression, 113
Greene, Jamal, 14
Grewal, David, 60

Hale, Robert, 17, 27
Hand, Learned, 100, 177n63
hands-tying, 80–81
harmonization, legal, 89, 92–93, 96, 173n17, 173n26
Harris, Cheryl, 73
Hart, Oliver, 34
Hayek, Friedrich, 13
Hesselink, Martijn, 120–21, 123, 124
historical materialism, 24, 26, 37–38

Hobbes, Thomas, 67
Hockett, Robert, 76
Hodgson, Geoffrey, 18
Homestead Act (1862), 72
hostage taking, 80
human capabilities approach, 15–16, 125–37
Hungary, 22

inalienability rule, 53–54
India, 56–57
indigenous peoples, 48
individual autonomy: as obstacle to social justice, 4; private law grounded in, 9–10, 44; privileged by capitalist law, 3, 4; property linked to, 50. *See also* private actors; private law
inequalities: and legal arbitrage, 12, 43–44, 85, 90, 95–97, 99; and legal empowerment, 43–44, 48, 51, 63
injury, legal, 51, 52, 70
institutionalism, 16–19, 26–27, 29
intellectual property, 38, 46, 47, 49, 88, 107
international law, 76, 89, 96, 130
International Monetary Fund (IMF), 8–9, 92
international private law, 91–92
Italy, 61

Japan, 55–56, 106
Jim Crow system, 73
justice. *See* social justice; substantive justice
just private-law code (JPL), 124–25, 129–32

Kessler, Jeremy, 36–38
Keynes, John Maynard, 7

Keynesianism, 16–17, 23, 30
Kornai, Janos, 181n1
Kusiak, Joanna, 103

labor: free movement of, 63; laws related to, 10, 12, 14, 29, 47, 68–69, 160n34; in Marxist conception of capitalism, 16–17, 34, 45, 61, 64; property in relation to, 49; temporary, 63–64, 165n97; unionization of, 10, 14, 47, 61–64, 164n87
law and political economy (LPE), 36, 156n59
law/legal regime: capitalism as legal regime, 1–7, 10–11, 23, 37–39, 102, 109–13, 117, 137–39; capitalism's use of, ix–x, 2, 11–12, 23; centralized vs. decentralized, 29; change accomplished through, x, 4, 36, 38, 109–16, 123–24, 129–30, 134–35, 137–38, 141–43; choice of, 89, 93–99, 175n45; freedom and, 36; harmonization of, 89, 92–93, 96, 173n17, 173n26; incompleteness/interpretability of, 12, 83–85, 88; independence of, from political/moral influences, 119, 122; legitimacy of, 4–5, 41, 70, 100, 141; moral basis needed for, 122, 124; neutrality imputed to, 7, 24, 27, 79; norms in relation to, ix–x, 4, 13, 15, 19, 27, 33, 79–80, 88, 96–97, 100, 111–12, 116, 137–38; pluralism in, 83–84, 88–96; purposes of, 12, 30, 88, 100; role of power in, 35–37; rule of law and, 22, 58, 150n58, 177n64; social systems in relation to, 19; standards and rules in, 84–85; theories of, 35–37; who benefits from, 19, 41, 74, 100. *See also* capitalist law; civil law; common law; private law; public law; Roman law
legal arbitrage, 83–101; in capitalist law, 89, 99–101; capitalist uses of, 3, 12–13, 43; defending against, 88, 95–96; defined, x, 83; financial/legal inequalities as factor in use of, 12, 43–44, 85, 90, 95–97, 99; at the global level, 90–96; individual autonomy privileged over rights by, 3; institutional change resulting from, 87; mobility as factor in, 98–99; opportunities for, 12, 83–84, 87–88, 90–91, 97, 99; by private actors, 12; and public law, 96–99; standards and rules as factors in, 84–85; and taxes, 85–86, 99–100; unintended consequences resulting from, 86–87; who benefits from, 12, 86–87, 90, 95–96, 96–101. *See also* legal empowerment
legal empowerment, 41–65; appropriation of resources by means of, 2–3; colonialism and, 6; constraints on capitalism fought by means of, 11–13, 35, 40; contracts and, 60–65; of corporations, 10–11, 68; critique of, 43–44; financial assets and, 8; financial inequalities affecting, 43–44, 48, 51, 63; of private actors, ix, 2–4, 9, 11, 14–16, 35, 41–43, 64–65, 139–40; property and, 44–59. *See also* legal arbitrage
legal realism, 26, 27, 36

legitimacy: of coercion, 28, 66; of law, 4–5, 41, 70, 100, 141; of rights, 73
Levy, Jonathan, 35
liability rule, 53–55. *See also* limited liability; pollution, liability for
limited liability, 45–46, 132–33, 139–40
litigation: arbitration vs., 77–79; financial/legal resources required for, 15, 74, 82, 85, 97, 140; legislation as corrective for, 123; as means of access to coercive powers, 11; new issues arising in the course of, 123–24; strategic uses of, 43, 82, 97. *See also* class-action suits
Locke, John, 49
Luhmann, Niklas, 111–14, 122
Lyft, 124

market. *See* economy/market
Marx, Karl, 1, 2, 5, 7, 16–17, 24, 45, 49, 61, 64, 103
Marxism: critique of capitalism from standpoint of, 16–17, 27, 40, 103, 109; and institutionalism, 18; and legal theory, 21, 27, 37; priority of material/economic conditions in, 16, 21, 30, 109, 137
Melamed, Douglas, 53–54
Merkel, Angela, 145n12
Metzger, Ernest, 71
Michaels, Ralf, 175n45
minimal historical materialist account of law (MHMAL), 36–38
Minsky, Hyman, 17, 181n1
money and money creation, 76, 110, 117, 135–37

Moore, John, 34
moral basis of law, 122
Moyn, Samuel, 36–38
Mullenix, Linda, 74
multinational corporations, 11, 62–63
Musk, Elon, 62, 93, 164n87

National Conference of State Legislatures, 173n17
National Housing Act (1934), 113
National Labor Relations Act (1935), 61, 113
National Labor Relations Board, 68
nature: capitalism's use and abuse of, 3, 5, 39–40, 102; controversy over granting rights to, 73; property rights and, 45. *See also* climate change; pollution, liability for; state of nature
neoliberalism, 18, 21, 58
Netherlands, 54–55, 64, 94, 105, 109
new comparative economics, 29–30
New Deal, 8, 113–14
new institutional economics, 29, 87
Nigeria, 54–55, 132
norms: of capitalism, 20; coercion guided by, 41; democratic, 14–15, 33, 35; law in relation to, ix–x, 4, 13, 15, 19, 27, 33, 79–80, 88, 96–97, 100, 111–12, 116, 137–38; plurality of, 89–90; of private law, 117, 121, 124–25, 137, 142; of public law, 117
North, Douglass, 18, 31, 141
nuisance law, 52
Nussbaum, Martha, 15, 125, 127–29

Omarova, Saule, 76
Organisation for Economic Co-operation and Development (OECD), 61, 64

Padgett, John, 104–5, 113
Panama Papers, 99
Pandora Papers, 99
Paradise Papers, 99
partnerships, 85–86
Pashukanis, Evgeny, 7, 24–27, 35, 117, 139, 153n21
path dependence, 18, 30, 87
Peari, Sagi, 98–99
Pennsylvania Coal Company, 51–52
Pettit, Philip, 31
piercing the corporate veil, 55, 133
Piketty, Thomas, 146n15
Poland, 22
Polanyi, Karl, x, 6, 22
pollution, liability for, 54, 59, 96, 130–32
populism, 5, 22, 108, 180n26
positivism, 88
Posner, Eric, 158n10
Poulantzas, Nicos, 27–29, 31–32, 37, 40
power: defined, 41; Enlightenment concern with, 15; institutions in relation to, 19; justification of private, 119–20; in law, 35–37; property imbricated with, 33–34; social justice and, x–xi, 15. *See also* coercion, powers of legal; domination; legal empowerment
precautionary principle, 96, 131
privacy, 70
private actors: access of, to legal coercion, ix, 3, 11–13, 67, 69–75, 79, 82, 140; legal arbitrage by, 12; legal empowerment of, ix, 2–4, 9, 11, 14–16, 35, 41–43, 64–65, 139–40; protection of, from state power, 23, 32–33; rights of others as constraint on, 15. *See also* individual autonomy; private law
private law: absence of constraints on, 14–16, 119; capitalist privileging of, over public, 2–4, 6, 11, 16, 26, 35, 117; capitalist use of, 2, 23, 35, 114; colonialism and, 6; core characteristics of, ix–x, 11; critique of, 43–44, 120–22; defined, 9, 10, 42–43, 139; democratization of, 33, 116, 120–25, 137; divergent views of, 9–11; European code (EPL-code) for, 121, 123, 182n13; human capabilities approach to, 125–37; individual autonomy as ground of, 9–10, 44; just private-law code (JPL), 124–25, 129–32; norms of, 117, 121, 124–25, 137, 142; people disadvantaged by, 2–4, 6, 8, 11, 15–16; portability of, 96; property as exemplary case of, 44–59; public law in relation to, ix–x, 4, 9–10, 12–13, 22–23, 139; reform of, 124–38; regulatory controls and, 9; the state in relation to, 32–33, 118–19. *See also* capitalist law; individual autonomy; legal empowerment; private actors
private sphere. *See* public vs. private spheres
procedural rules, 67, 72, 75–77, 79, 135

property: abstract conception of, 46; capitalism linked to, 45; in capitalist regimes, 25, 34; communal stewardship of, 45; conflicts involving, 50–55; contracts compared to, 60; creditors' rights concerning others', 42; critique of, 47; in England, 52–53; exploitation for value linked to conception of, 48–49; in India, 56–57; justification of, 120; labor in relation to, 49; modern vs. ancient conceptions of, 46; nature and, 45; origin of rights of, 55–59; power imbricated with, 33–34; race and gender as factors in the right to own, 72; relational/social aspects of, 24–25, 33–34, 47, 55–59; rights associated with, 23, 44–59, 181n6; slaves as, 68; in South Africa, 57–59; tangible and intangible, 45–46, 49–50. *See also* intellectual property
property (veto) rule, 52–54
prostitution, 69
public law: boundaries of, 96; capitalist privileging of private law over, 2–4, 6, 11, 16, 26, 35, 117; constraints on, 14–15; defined, 9, 139; economic development fostered by, 117–18; legal arbitrage and, 96–99; norms of, 117; private law in relation to, ix–x, 4, 9–10, 12–13, 22–23, 139; protections offered to capitalism by, 2; regulatory controls and, 9, 40
public vs. private spheres, 127–28

Rawls, John, 43
redistribution, 12, 33–34, 55–58, 97

regulation: arbitrage and, 83; and private law, 8; and public law, 8; of securities, 98–99; the state and, 8–9
remedies, legal, 69–72, 167n22
Renner, Karl, 24–25
responsibility. *See* "take responsibility" principle
rights: of corporations, 14, 34, 35, 73, 126, 133; failure of legal systems based on, 14; human capabilities approach in relation to, 125–29; individual, 44–45; legal arbitrage's privileging of individual autonomy over, 3; legal claims dependent on possession of, 72–75; legitimacy of, 73; "natural" status granted to individual/property, 23; norms vs., 13; positive vs. negative, 127; race and gender as factors in possessing, 72–73; remedies associated with, 69–72, 167n22. *See also* individual autonomy
Roman law, 26, 41, 42, 44, 46, 71, 162n56, 167n22, 181n6
Romano, Roberta, 98
Royal Dutch Shell. *See* Shell
rule of law, 22, 58, 150n58, 177n64

Sanderson case (1868), 51–52
Scalia, Antonin, 77–78
Schumpeter, Joseph, 1
Scott, Alan, 32
Securities Exchange Act (1934), 113
securities regulation, 98–99, 172n16
Sen, Amartya, 15, 125–27
shadow banking, 76, 80, 106, 118

Index / 194

shareholders, of corporations, 45–46, 49, 54, 132–33, 139
Shell, 54–55, 132
Shklar, Judith, 28
slavery, 68, 72
smart contracts, 81–82
social contract, 124
socialism: capitalism vs., 102; failures of, 19, 103; legal theory and, 7, 24, 27; transition to capitalism from, 21–22
social justice: as basis of legal regime, 19, 122; human capabilities approach and, 128; individual license as obstacle to, 4, 100; power and, x–xi, 15
Social Security Act (1935), 113
soft law, 89, 92, 173n26
Sotomayor, Sonia, 71
South Africa, 57–59
South Carolina, 94
Soviet Union, 19, 21, 24, 27, 103
special-purpose acquisition companies (SPACs), 94–95
Spokeo v. Robins, 70–71
Stalinism, 27
standing rules, 70
state: capitalism coextensive with the modern, 5–6, 11; checks and balances in, ix, 4, 14, 41, 67, 139; coercion/violence used by, 11, 28, 41, 66–67; conceptions of, 30–32; constraints on, 23, 32–33, 67–68; the economy/market in relation to, 5–6, 17, 21–22, 29–30, 32–33; franchising of coercive power by, 76; individual rights in relation to, 127; private law in relation to, 32–33; regulatory, 8–9. *See also* failed states
state of nature, 80–81

Streeck, Wolfgang, 18, 87
subjective law, 26, 153n21
substantive justice, 122–23
Sunstein, Cass, 162n52
Suri, Siddharth, 64
Sweden, 62

"take responsibility" principle, 132–35, 139, 142
tax arbitrage, 85–86, 99–100
Tesla, 62–63, 93
Texas, 93–94
Thatcher, Margaret, 145n12
Thelen, Kathleen, 87
Tilly, Charles, 31, 66
tort law, 55, 69, 89, 93–94, 96, 120, 130–31, 139
tragedy of the commons, 45
treaty law, 89
Treaty of Rome, 63
Trump, Donald, 164n87, 180n26
Tusk, Donald, 180n26

Uber, 64, 124
Unger, Roberto, 36, 38
U.N. Global Compact, 130
United Automobile Workers (UAW), 164n87
United Kingdom: corporate law in, 54–55, 94, 132; as a leading capitalist economy, 7, 9, 22, 57, 62, 95, 106; and populism, 180n26
United States: and conflict of laws, 89, 92–94; harmonization of laws in, 173n17, 173n26; as a leading capitalist economy, 7, 9, 22, 57, 62, 95, 106; and undocumented immigrants, 98; unions in, 47, 61–62
U.S. Bill of Rights, 44
U.S. Chamber of Commerce, 75

U.S. Congress, 71, 75, 85
U.S. Constitution, 48, 70, 93. *See also* U.S. Bill of Rights
U.S. Supreme Court, 14, 47, 70, 75, 77–78, 160n34
utopianism, 19, 37, 128

Veblen, Thorstein, 17, 29
Venkatesan, Rashmi, 57
veto rule. *See* property (veto) rule

Waldron, Jeremy, 150n58, 177n64
Walmart, 81
Washington Consensus, 155n49
Weber, Max, 17, 31–32, 42
Werbach, Kevin, 81
Weyl, Glen, 158n10
Williamson, Oliver, 18
World Bank, 58, 92, 155n49

Zuckerberg, Mark, 132